*Bristol City Football Club
An A-Z*

Bristol City Football Club
An A-Z

Dean Hayes

Aureus

First Published 2001

©2001 Dean Hayes

Dean Hayes has asserted the Author's right under the Copyright, Designs and Patents Act 1988 to be identified as Author of this Work.

All rights reserved. No part of this publication may be reproduced, stored in a retrieval system, or transmitted, in any form or by any means, electronic, mechanical, photocopying or otherwise, without the prior permission of Aureus Publishing.

This publication has not been endorsed or approved by Bristol City Football Club and is in no way connected to the club.

Front cover: John Ateyo, the greatest goalscorer in Bristol City Football Club's history and the holder of the Robins' appearance record.

ISBN 1 899750 07 X

Printed in Great Britain.

A catalogue record for this book is available from the British Library.

Aureus Publishing Limited, 24 Mafeking Road, Cardiff, CF23 5DQ, UK.
Tel: (029) 2045 5200 Fax: (029) 2045 5200
Int. tel: +44 29 2045 5200 Int. fax: +44 29 2045 5200
E-mail: sales@aureus.co.uk
           meuryn.hughes@aureus.co.uk
Web site: www.aureus.co.uk

A

ABANDONED MATCHES

An abandoned match may be defined as one which is called off by the referee whilst it is in progress because conditions do not permit it to be completed. Far fewer matches are abandoned in modern times because if there is some doubt about the possibility of playing the full game, the match is more likely to be postponed.

Below is a full list of abandoned matches involving the Robins.

Date	Opponents	Venue	Score	Reason
10.11.1898	Corinthians	Away	1-1	Bad Light (75 mins)
22.12.1900	Watford	Away	0-0	Fog(75 mins)
16.11.1901	Bristol Rovers	Away	0-2	Fog(80 mins)
14.12.1901	Gainsborough.T.	Home	2-1	Bad Light (45 mins)
18.11.1916	Bath City	Away	4-0	Bad Light (85 mins)
24.11.1917	Royal Engineers	Home	1-1	Bad Light (82 mins)
15.02.1919	Bristol Dockers*	Home	6-0	Crowd Invasion (85mins)
16.04.1923	Bristol Rovers	Home	3-1	Bad Light (80 mins)
21.12.1935	Crystal Palace	Home	1-1	Fog (83 mins)
14.09.1940	Walsall*	Home	2-0	Air Raid (32 mins)
23.02.1957	Liverpool	Away	1-0	Waterlogged (45 mins)
28.01.1961	Leicester City	Away	0-0	Waterlogged (45 mins)
26.12.1963	Q.P.R.	Home	3-0	Fog (45 mins)
20.01.1973	Sheffield Wed	Away	0-0	Snow and Ice (55 mins)
04.12.1976	Leeds United	Home	0-0	Fog (45 mins)
08.01.1994	Liverpool	Home	1-1	Floodlight Failure (65 mins)

* Results allowed to stand.

AGGREGATE SCORES
Bristol City's highest aggregate score in any competition came in the Football League Cup of 1988-89 against Oxford United. The Robins won the first match at the Manor Ground 4-2 and then beat the U's in the return match at Ashton Gate 2-0 to win the second round tie 6-2. City then went on to reach the semi-finals before losing to Nottingham Forest.

AGOSTINO, PAUL
Australian international Paul Agostino was signed from Young Boys of Berne during the summer of 1995 after having a ten-day trial at Ashton Gate the previous campaign. Earlier in his career, he had impressed as a 16-year-old with West Adelaide in the Australian Premier League and helped his country reach the Youth World Cup semi-finals.

He made his City debut in a 1-1 draw at home to Blackpool on the opening day of the 1995-96 season, during which he formed an exciting striking partnership with fellow Australian David Seal. Towards the end of that season he won his first full cap for Australia when he came on as a substitute against Chile. In 1996-97 Seal was confined to the Reserves for much of the campaign and so Agostino formed a new and excellent partnership with Shaun Goater. He scored four goals in the 9-2 FA Cup win over St Albans but at the end of the season in which he had taken his tally of goals to 26 in 102 games, he exercised his rights under freedom of contract and signed for the German club, Munich 1860.

AIZLEWOOD, MARK
Mark Aizlewood followed his elder brother Steve to Newport County, making his league debut as a 16-year-old schoolboy after getting permission from his headteacher. He won Welsh Schoolboy and Under-23 honours before a £50,000 move to Luton Town. Another £50,000 deal took him to Charlton Athletic in November 1982 and he was their Player of the Year in 1984-85 and 1985-86. He had won ten full Welsh caps by the end of 1987-88 but at the end of the following season he was stripped of the captaincy and transferred to Bradford City for £200,000. He left Valley Parade in August 1990 to join Bristol City for £125,000.

He made his debut at home to Blackburn Rovers on the opening day of the 1990-91 season, scoring the Robins first goal in a 4-2 win. His only other goal in that campaign proved to be the winner at Millwall. He starred in the club's

FA Cup run in 1991-92 as City beat Wimbledon and Leicester City before losing to Nottingham Forest. He had scored three goals in 112 League and Cup games when he was transferred to Cardiff City in October 1993.

At Ninian Park he won the last of his 39 Welsh caps before leaving to become player-coach at Merthyr Tydfil.

Mark Aizlewood

AKINBIYI, ADE

Ade Akinbiyi began his league career with Norwich City, breaking into the first team at the end of the 1993-94 season. He spent a beneficial loan period at Brighton, scoring four goals in seven games before returning to Carrow Road. Though he proved to be a prolific scorer in the Canaries' Reserve side, he was given few opportunities in the first team and in January 1997 he was transferred to Gillingham for £250,000.

He was the Gill's top-scorer in 1997-98, a feat which prompted Bristol City to pay a club record £1.2 million for his services in May 1998. He made his debut in a 2-2 home draw against Oxford United on the opening day of the 1998-99 season. Akinbiyi not only topped the club's scoring charts with 19 league goals but surprised everyone with his phenomenal work-rate.

A great favourite with the Ashton Gate fans, he was transferred to Wolverhampton Wanderers for £3.5 million in September 1999.

ALLISON, WAYNE

Wayne Allison began his career with Halifax Town, making his league debut for the Shaymen prior to turning professional in the summer of 1987. His performances led to Watford paying £250,000 for his services in July 1989 but after failing to secure a regular spot in the Hornets' side, he left Vicarage Road a year later to join Bristol City in exchange for Mark Gavin.

He made his City debut as a substitute for Bob Taylor in a 2-2 draw at West Bromwich Albion in a Rumbelows Cup tie before scoring on his full league debut against Port Vale on 27 October 1990. Allison was the club's leading scorer for three of the next four seasons with a best of 15 in 1993-94, a campaign in which he scored a hat-trick in the 3-0 home win over Birmingham City. He had scored 55 goals in 217 League and Cup games when he joined Swindon Town for £475,000 in July 1995.

In his first season at the County Ground, Allison was the Wiltshire club's top-scorer as they won the Second Division Championship. Top-scorer again the following season, his home-town club Huddersfield Town paid £800,000 to take him to Yorkshire in November 1997.

The big front man scored 19 goals in 80 games for the Terriers, though his unselfish play created many more for Marcus Stewart. Allison left the McAlpine Stadium in the summer of 1999 and joined Tranmere Rovers.

Wayne Allison

ANDERSON, BOB

Following RAF service, Durham-born goalkeeper Bob Anderson joined Middlesbrough in November 1945 but after just one league appearance, he moved to Crystal Palace following a short spell with Blackhall Colliery FC. Anderson went on to make 38 league appearances for the Selhurst Park club but in March 1953 he joined Bristol Rovers as a replacement for Bert Hoyle who had been injured in a road accident. He played 10 games that season as Rovers won the Third Division (South) Championship but in April 1954 Bristol City manager Pat Beasley brought him to Ashton Gate.

He made his debut for the Robins on Christmas Day 1954 deputising for the injured Tony Cook in a 2-1 win over Reading. He kept his place and went on to play in 23 games as City won the Third Division (South) Championship. In fact, the Ashton Gate club were undefeated in Anderson's last 18 appearances that season. Anderson went on to play in 115 games for the club before a back injury forced his retirement in 1961.

ANGLO-ITALIAN CUP

When Swindon Town won the Football League Cup in 1969 they were ineligible for the Fairs Cup because they were not a First Division side. Consequently they organised a match against the Italian League Cup winners, AS Roma and played for the Anglo-Italian League Cup. The following year the Anglo-Italian Cup was introduced for club sides from the two countries who had no involvement in Europe.

Bristol City did not enter the competition until 1992-93 when after beating Watford (Home 1-0) and drawing with Luton Town (Away 1-1) they qualified for the international stage of the competition. Their results were as follows:

Cosenza (Home) 0-2	Pisa (Away) 3-4
Reggiana (Home) 1-2	Cremonese (Away) 2-2

In 1993-94 the Robins lost 3-1 at Portsmouth and beat Oxford United 2-1 at Ashton Gate with goals from Allison and Rosenoir but failed to qualify for the international stages.

ANGLO-SCOTTISH CUP

The Anglo-Scottish Cup was inaugurated in 1975-76 following the withdrawal of Texaco from the competition of that name. Bristol City lost their first-ever match in the competition 1-0 at Chelsea but though they later drew with Fulham (Away 2-2) and beat Norwich City (Home 4-1) they failed to qualify for the knockout stages.

In 1976-77 the Robins again failed to reach the two-legged knockout stage against Scottish opposition despite beating West Bromwich Albion (Home 1-0) and Notts County (Home 2-0) in their group games. Their undoing came in their final group game when they lost 4-2 at Nottingham Forest.

In 1977-78 City went all the way to the Anglo-Scottish Cup Final. Despite losing 1-0 at Birmingham City, the Robins beat Bristol Rovers 3-1 courtesy of a Tom Ritchie hat-trick and Plymouth Argyle 2-0 to qualify for the knockout stages. After losing 2-0 at Partick Thistle, two goals from Jimmy Mann and one from Clive Whitehead gave City a 3-2 aggregate win. In the semi-finals, the Robins beat Hibernian 6-4 on aggregate to set up a two-legged final against St Mirren. Goals from Cormack and Mabbutt helped City win the first leg at Love Street 2-1 whilst Mabbutt was again on target at Ashton Gate as the clubs played out a 1-1 draw, giving the Robins the trophy 3-2 on aggregate.

In 1978-79 the Robins won all their group games - Bristol Rovers (Home 6-1) Cardiff City (Home 1-0) and Fulham (Away 3-0) but then lost 4-3 on aggregate to St Mirren who gained some revenge for defeat in the previous season's final.

In 1979-80 City again reached the final, beating Birmingham City (Away 4-0) and Fulham (Home 1-0) and drawing with Plymouth Argyle (Away 0-0) in their group matches. Partick Thistle were beaten 3-1 on aggregate and Morton 3-2 as City went through to face old rivals St Mirren in the final. The Scottish side won both matches, beating the Robins 5-1 on aggregate.

The club last entered the competition in 1980-81 but failed to qualify for the knockout stages after the following group results - Fulham (Home 2-0) Notts County (Home 1-1) and Orient (Away 0-1)

ANNAN, ARCHIE

Scottish right-back Archie Annan played his early football with West Calder and St Bernard's before joining Sunderland in July 1903. His stay at Roker Park was brief and towards the end of that year he moved to Sheffield United. In April 1905 he followed Harry Thickett to Ashton Gate for £200, making his debut in a 5-1 defeat at Manchester United on the opening day of the 1905-06 season. Annan was an ever-present in his first two seasons with City, making 77

11

consecutive league appearances from his debut. He went on to appear in 161 League and Cup games for the Robins before leaving to play for Burslem Port Vale in the summer of 1911.

After just one season at Vale Park, a campaign in which he was hampered by injuries, he left to become manager of Mid-Rhondda. After the First World War he returned to Ashton Gate to become City's coach, a position he held for five years.

APPEARANCES

John Ateyo holds the record for the greatest number of appearances in a Bristol City shirt, with a total of 645 games to his credit between 1951 and 1966. Ateyo played 596 league games, 41 FA Cup games, six Football League Cup games and two miscellaneous cup games.

The players with the highest number of appearances for Bristol City are as follows:

		League	*FA Cup*	*Lg Cup*	*Others*	*Total*
1.	John Ateyo	596	41	6	2	645
2.	Trevor Tainton	448(30)	31	35(3)	34	548(33)
3.	Tom Ritchie	401(14)	24(2)	27(1)	35	487(17)
4.	Gerry Sweeney	397(10)	23	27	33	480(10)
5.	Rob Newman	382(12)	27	30(1)	31	470(13)
6.	Gerry Gow	368(7)	17	27(2)	22(2)	434(11)
7.	Geoff Merrick	361(6)	16(1)	30	20	427(6)
8.	Ivor Guy	404	22	0	0	426
9.	Mike Thresher	379	29	6	1	415
10.	Jack Connor	354(1)	35	16	2	407(1)

ARMSTRONG, DICK

After impressing in non-League football with Willington and Easington Colliery, inside-forward Dick Armstrong was given his chance at league level with Nottingham Forest. However, much of his time at the City Ground was spent in the club's reserve side and in May 1935, City manager Bob Hewison brought him to Ashton Gate.

He made his City debut in a 2-0 win at Watford on the opening day of the 1935-36 season, a campaign in which he was the club's top-scorer with 11 goals.

Later in his Ashton Gate career, he reverted to wing-half and in 1937-38 turned in some memorable performances as City finished runners-up in the Third Division (South). Armstrong went on to score 18 goals in 115 League and Cup games and though he was on the club's books until March 1944, he only appeared in 18 wartime games.

ASHTON GATE

Ashton Gate was inaugurated in September 1896 when the area now used for football was first used for a cricket game involving Gloucestershire and Somerset. The Bedminster Athletic Ground though was also used for football and in March 1899 housed its first international when England played Wales.

After Bedminster had agreed to become junior partners in a merger with Bristol City, the club began to make changes to the ground that they now called Ashton Gate. The first change was to move the pitch some 50 yards to its current position and then after moving Bedminster's original stand to the east side to become 'Number Two Stand' built a new 'Number One Stand' on the west side.

Ashton Gate housed another football international against Wales in 1913 after having staged a Rugby Union international between England and Wales some five years earlier. Though the club had a successful period around this time, winning the Second Division Championship in 1905-06 and reaching the FA Cup Final three years later, it couldn't be sustained and in 1928, City had to sell two of its players to finance the Covered End terrace at the Winterstoke Road end of the ground!

In 1929 much of the Number Two Stand was destroyed by fire whilst four years later the club came very close to selling Ashton Gate to the local council for £16,000, provided they were granted a long lease for an annual rent of £640. Thankfully the council declined the offer.

In January 1941, the Number Two Stand was destroyed in a series of air raids and though the War Damages Commission gave £16,500 towards rebuilding costs by the time of its completion in 1953, the costs had spiralled to £30,000.

The club's chairman, Harry Dolman, who was an engineer, was responsible for designing the first floodlights at Ashton Gate. They were first used for a friendly against Wolverhampton Wanderers in January 1953, though after 12 years of constant use, they were sold to Burton Albion. Later in that year of 1965, the Robins' new floodlights were switched on, also against the Molineux club.

In 1966, the Number Two Stand was demolished and this allowed the occupants of a block of flats that had been built on the site of Bedminster's first pitch, a clear view of the Ashton Gate playing area!

In 1970, the Harry Dolman stand was built at a cost of £235,000, four times the original estimate. To pay off the debt the Robins had to sell all their club houses and obtain pledges from the FA and various sponsors.

The stand was in full use during the club's four years in the top flight but after they had plummeted to the League's basement, the 1897 company was wound up in 1982.

When Ashton Gate was inspected under the Safety of Sports Grounds Act, the grounds capacity of 30,868 remained unchanged, though the Taylor Report did reduce it to 25,271. It was 1991 when the club decided to go ahead with the first stage of making Ashton Gate an all-seater stadium.

Seats were installed on the terracing of both the Covered End and Grandstand Paddock and the grandstand roof extended to cover the new seats. New floodlights were also installed along the front of both side stand roofs and all this work cost £700,000. It was later discovered that proper tendering procedures for the

Ashton Gate

£459,000 Football Trust grant had not been followed ! The club's chairman was banned by the FA for nine months and the club fined £40,000. The second phase of the post-Taylor work saw the construction of a stand at the Open End on Ashton Road, which after objections from local residents had to be reduced from a double-decker to single tier stand.

Now with a capacity of 21,479, Ashton Gate remains by far the best Football League ground in the south-west.

ASHTON GATE EIGHT

Bristol City overstretched themselves during their time in the First Division (1976-77 to 1979-80) and could not afford their wage bill as the team slid back down the League. In October 1981 following their relegation from the Second Division, they were £700,000 in debt (with £120,000 tax outstanding) and losing £3,000 per week. In the week before Christmas that year, one of their directors resigned in order to make way for two local businessmen, who promised to raise £500,000 to save the club. But with City still anchored at the foot of the Third Division, it still wasn't enough and manager Bob Houghton resigned.

Accountants were then called in and their solution was drastic. They gave eight players, whose wages were costing a staggering £250,000 a year, immediate free transfer. These players were Peter Aitken, Chris Garland, Jimmy Mann, Julian Marshall, Geoff Merrick, David Rodgers, Gerry Sweeney and Trevor Tainton. They used the PFA to try to improve City's offer of compensation but the writing was on the wall when on 26 January 1982, the club's chairman said Bristol City would go out of business in a fortnight if agreement was not reached.

Finally on 3 February 1982, the 'Ashton Gate Eight' as they became known, bowed to the inevitable and allowed their contracts to be cancelled, clearing the way for the Robins to be reborn from the ashes, although sadly, too late to prevent relegation to the Fourth Division.

ASSOCIATE MEMBERS CUP

The early rounds of this competition announced by the Football League in December 1983, were run on knockout lines and played on a regional basis. One of the founder entrants, Bristol City were placed in the Southern Section but went out of the competition at the first hurdle, losing 3-1 at Exeter City.

ATEYO, JOHN

The greatest goalscorer in the club's history and the holder of the Robins' appearance record, John Ateyo was playing in the Wiltshire League for Westbury United when he signed amateur forms for Portsmouth. He made two First Division appearances for Pompey, who were keen to obtain his signature but the Fratton Park club's insistence that he lived locally allowed Bristol City in the shape of chairman Harry Dolman to step in and sign him.

He scored on his Robins' debut in a 3-1 home win over Newport County on the opening day of the 1951-52 season. After scoring the first of 16 hat-tricks for the club against Swindon Town (Home 5-1) on 20 February 1954, he won selection for the FA XI, quickly followed by England Under-23 and England 'B' caps. He made his full international debut for England against Spain at Wembley on 30 November 1955 when he scored in England's 4-1 win. Further caps followed against Brazil, Sweden, Republic of Ireland and Denmark until May 1957 when he made his last appearance in a World Cup qualifying match against the Republic of Ireland in Dublin. Ateyo scored to take his tally to five goals in six games, helping England to progress to the final stages of the competition in Sweden.

Ateyo was City's leading scorer in 11 of his 15 seasons at Ashton Gate, with a best of 29 goals in 1955-56, a total which included hat-tricks in the wins over Bury (Home 3-1) and Lincoln City (Home 5-1). Bury were City's opponents on 16 March 1957 when Ateyo scored the Robins' quickest-ever goal after just nine seconds!

When the Robins beat Chichester City 11-0 in the first round of the 1960-61 FA Cup competition, John Ateyo scored five of the goals. His career total of 30 FA Cup goals was the highest in the competition until Denis Law overtook his record.

Despite the interest of a number of bigger clubs like Chelsea and Liverpool, Ateyo remained loyal to Bristol City. Throughout most of his Ashton Gate career he was a part-time professional, firstly qualifying as a quantity surveyor and later as a teacher. His loyalty to the Robins was rewarded with a testimonial match in October 1966 when Leeds United visited Ashton Gate.

Ateyo, who scored 351 goals in 645 games for the Robins, died of a heart attack in June 1993.

ATTENDANCE - AVERAGE
The average home league attendances of Bristol City over the last ten seasons have been as follows:

1990-91	13,495	1995-96	7,017
1991-92	11,479	1996-97	10,802
1992-93	11,004	1997-98	11,846
1993-94	8,852	1998-99	12,860
1994-95	8,005	1999-00	9,803

ATTENDANCE - HIGHEST
The record attendance at Ashton Gate is 43,335 for the fifth round FA Cup game with Preston North End on 16 February 1935. The game was goalless but City lost the replay at Deepdale nine days later 5-0. However, over 50,000 were judged to be in the ground on 30 January 1935 for the fourth round replay against Portsmouth, when the gates were rushed and the crowd broke in. The official attendance was given as 42,885.

ATTENDANCES - LOWEST
The lowest attendance at Ashton Gate for a first-class match is 1,515 for the Anglo-Italian Cup game against Oxford United on 7 September 1993. For the record, the Robins won 2-1.

AUTOWINDSCREEN SHIELD
The Autowindscreen Shield replaced the Autoglass Trophy for the 1994-95 season. The Robins first participated in the competition the following season when despite losing their first group match 3-0 at Oxford United, they qualified for the knockout stages with a 2-0 home defeat of Barnet in their second group match. After a staunch rearguard action at Gay Meadow produced a goalless draw in the first round match against Shrewsbury Town, City went out of the competition after losing 7-6 on penalties.

In 1996-97 the Autowindscreen Shield became a straight knockout competition but after beating Swansea City at the Vetch Field 1-0 City lost 2-1 at Watford in the Southern Area quarter-final. In 1997-98 the Robins beat Millwall 1-0 but then lost by a similar score at Bournemouth again in the Southern Area quarter-final.

The Robins won their way through to the final of the 1999-2000 final at Wembley where their opponents were Stoke City. Kavanagh gave the Potters the lead in the 32nd minute when he charged in to the area to hammer the ball inside Mercer's near post. Brian Tinnion hit Stoke's bar before Paul Holland's diving header went in off substitute Damien Spencer to equalise. Peter Thorne scored a controversial winner in the 82nd minute to give Stoke the trophy. Stoke's Hansson took a quick free-kick whilst the Robins were regrouping and Graham Kavanagh crossed for Peter Thorne to score. Bristol City boss Tony Fawthorp was fuming because the referee was lecturing the City wall when the free-kick was taken!

AWAY MATCHES

Bristol City's best away win is 8-2 at Walsall on 26 February 1938 when Alf Rowles scored a hat-trick. The Robins have also scored seven goals away from home on four occasions, beating Aberdare Athletic 7-3 in 1926-27, Kingstonian 7-1 in the FA Cup in 1933-34, Reading 7-2 in 1947-48 and Barnsley 7-4 in 1958-59. The Robins' worst defeat away from home was the 9-0 defeat at Coventry City on 28 April 1934.

AWAY SEASONS

The club's highest number of away wins came in season's 1905-06 and 1954-55 when they won 13 of their matches. In 1905-06 they achieved the feat from just 19 games in winning the Second Division Championship. In 1954-55 they played 23 matches but still ended the season as champions of the Third Division (South).

The club's fewest away wins (one) occurred in season's 1932-33, 1934-35, 1970-71 and 1980-81, although during City's Southern League days, they failed to win one single away game in 1899-1900 drawing seven and losing seven of their 14 matches.

B

BACON, FRANK
Director Frank Bacon took over at Bristol City in October 1910 following the surprise dismissal of Harry Thickett. Though he was essentially a stop-gap between Thickett and the third spell of Sam Hollis' managerial career at Ashton Gate, he proved to be a key figure in the signing of future England international, Billy Wedlock.

Bacon stayed in office until a shock 3-0 home defeat by non-League Crewe Alexandra in the first round of the FA Cup in January 1911.

BAILEY, JACK
Full-back Jack Bailey was spotted by Robins' manager Bob Hewison whilst playing for Bristol Aeroplane Company during the Second World War. He made his City debut in a 3-2 defeat at Cardiff City on 2 April 1945 and twelve days later played in the marathon War League cup tie at Ninian Park. Bailey made his Football League debut in a 4-3 defeat at Aldershot on the opening day of the 1946-47 season. With the exception of 1954-55 and 1955-56 when a broken arm reduced his number of appearances, Bailey missed very few games and was ever-present in 1947-48. His partnership with Ivor Guy was considered one of the best full-back pairings the club have ever had but after 396 League and Cup appearances for the Robins he left to play non-League football for Trowbridge Town. He later coached Welton Rovers before ending his involvement with the game.

Sadly, six months after retiring from working in the dispatch department of DRG Robinson's, Bailey died from a heart attack, a fate which also ended the life of his full-back partner Ivor Guy four months earlier.

BAILEY, JOHN
Liverpool-born left-back John Bailey began his career with Blackburn Rovers, for whom he made 120 league appearances during four seasons at Ewood Park.

John Bailey

He joined Everton in the summer of 1979 for a fee of £300,000 and was the club's only ever-present the following season as they struggled to avoid relegation. His form was such that within a year of his arrival at Goodison he had won England 'B' international honours. A firm favourite with the Everton fans, he helped the club win the FA Cup in 1984 when they beat Watford 2-0 at Wembley. But a few months later, he lost his regular full-back spot to Welsh international Pat Van Den Hauwe and in 1985 after appearing in 220 first team games, he was transferred to Newcastle United for a fee of £80,000.

In 1988 he left St James Park to join Bristol City on a free transfer. In his first season with the Robins, he helped them reach the Littlewood's League Cup semi-final and in 1989-90 promotion to the Second Division. It was during this latter season that he scored his only goal for the club in a 1-0 win at Crewe Alexandra. Bailey went on to make 104 League and Cup appearances for the Robins before returning to Goodison Park as Everton's 'B' team coach. A year later he was dismissed but wasn't out of the game long, taking up a coaching position with Sheffield United.

BANFIELD, LAURENCE

Tough-tackling left-back Laurence Banfield was signed from Paulton Rovers by City manager Sam Hollis in the summer of 1911.

After a season in the club's reserves, Banfield was given his first team debut in the final game of the 1911-12 season, a goalless draw at home to Hull City. Banfield was a virtual ever-present in the Robins' side, appearing in 99 games up until the outbreak of the First World War. When League football resumed in 1919-20, Banfield was still the club's first-choice left-back and was appointed captain, leading the club to the FA Cup semi-finals in that campaign. In December 1920 he was awarded a benefit game against Port Vale, a match which attracted a record crowd of 34,710 to Ashton Gate. After helping the club win the Third Division (South) Championship in 1922-23, Banfield who had scored seven goals in 281 games later held the position of player-manager of Ilfracombe Town.

BEASLEY, PAT

Pat Beasley joined his home-town club Stourbridge before being transferred to Arsenal as a 17-year-old in the summer of 1931. Playing primarily as a winger, he was restricted to reserve team football due to the consistency of Hulme and

Bastin but in 1933-34 he won a regular place and helped the club win the League Championship. In October 1936 he left Highbury to join Huddersfield Town where in the three seasons up to the outbreak of World War Two, he appeared in an FA Cup Final and won an England cap, scoring the winning goal against Scotland.

During the hostilities he 'guested' for Arsenal and won two wartime caps but in December 1945 he left Huddersfield to join Fulham. He helped the Cottagers win the Second Division Championship in 1948-49 but in the summer of 1950 he moved to Bristol City as the Ashton Gate club's player-manager.

He made his debut in a 1-0 defeat at Bournemouth on the opening day of the 1950-51 season, going on to score five goals in 66 games before retiring from playing just before his 40th birthday. The Robins won the Third Division (South) Championship under his managership in 1954-55 with 70 points but after two steady Second Division campaigns, his contract was terminated by mutual agreement in January 1958.

He then joined Birmingham City, initially as joint-manager with Arthur Turner but eight months later became acting manager and then team manager in January 1959. He left St Andrew's in May 1960 and after a spell as Fulham's scout, managed non-League Dover for four years.

BENNETT, WALTER

Hailing from a football family, his elder brother having played for Sheffield Wednesday in the 1890 FA Cup Final, Walter 'Cocky' Bennett began his career with his home-town club Mexborough Town. On joining Sheffield United, he scored in the Blades' 1899 FA Cup Final triumph, having helped the Yorkshire club win the League Championship in 1897-98. Whilst with United, Bennett won two full caps for England, appearing against Wales and Scotland in 1901.

In 1905, Bennett followed Harry Thickett to Ashton Gate and made his debut for his new club in a 1-0 home defeat at the hands of Liverpool.

When City won the Second Division Championship in 1905-06, Bennett, who scored 20 goals in 37 games, formed a good partnership with Willie Maxwell and Sammy Gilligan, the three players scoring 65 of City's 83 league goals. Included in Walter Bennett's total was a hat-trick in the 4-0 home win over Port Vale. Injuries reduced his number of appearances the following season but in May 1907 after scoring 22 goals in 49 games, he returned to his native Yorkshire to play for Denaby United.

He also worked at Denaby Main Colliery but in April 1908 he was tragically killed in a mining accident, being buried under tons of rocks.

BENT, JUNIOR

Huddersfield-born winger Junior Bent signed professional forms for his hometown club in December 1987 having already made his league debut in October of that year against Middlesbrough while still an apprentice. Though he had a spell as a regular in Town's Third Division side during 1988-89 he was generally on the fringe of first team action at Leeds Road. In November 1989 he joined Burnley on loan but in March 1990 he was transferred to Bristol City for £30,000.

On his arrival at Ashton Gate he found things tough and took some time to establish himself as a first team regular. He helped City beat top-flight sides Wimbledon and Liverpool in the FA Cup runs of 1991-92 and 1993-94. However, his most consistent season and his most successful as a goalscorer was 1994-95 but sadly his goals were not enough to prevent the Robins' relegation.

Loaned to Stoke City and Shrewsbury Town, he eventually left to join Blackpool in the summer of 1997 after having scored 23 goals in 211 League and Cup games for City.

BEST STARTS

Bristol City were unbeaten for the first 13 league games of the 1954-55 season when they won the Third Division (South) Championship. They won 10 and drew three of their fixtures before losing 3-2 at Southend United on 9 October 1954.

In 1902-03 and 1927-28 the Robins won each of their first five league games.

BOURTON, CLARRIE

Clarrie Bourton played his early football for Paulton Rovers while working as a printer. He joined Bristol City in the close season of 1927 but after only four first team games he left to join Blackburn Rovers in a deal which also took Albert Keating to Ewood Park and brought a fee of £3,650 to Ashton Gate. He scored 37 goals in 68 games for the Lancashire club before Harry Storer paid £750 to take him to Coventry City in the summer of 1931.

In his first season at Highfield Road he was the Football League's top goalscorer with 49 goals in 40 games. He scored in a club record 10 successive games, netted five goals in a 6-1 home win over Bournemouth and scored six hat-tricks. In 1932-33 he scored 40 goals in 39 league games and was second in the Football League charts to Hull City's Bill McNaughton. He continued to find the net with great regularity and helped Coventry win the Third Division (South) Championship in 1935-36. In six seasons at Highfield Road he scored 180 goals in 241 League and Cup games before leaving to play for Plymouth Argyle. Unable to settle at Home Park, he returned to play for Bristol City where in the 1938-39 season he was appointed caretaker-manager after Bob Hewison had been suspended by the FA for making illegal payments to amateurs. Scoring 14 goals in 60 games, he saw the Ashton Gate club into a respectable position in the top half of the table before reverting back to a non-managerial position when Hewison's suspension was lifted.

BOXLEY, JACK

Jack Boxley played his early football for Stourbridge, from where Bristol City manager Pat Beasley signed him in October 1950. The fast-raiding winger made his Robins' debut in a 2-1 home win over Newport County. The following season he suffered a serious leg injury that threatened his career but thankfully he recovered to serve the Ashton Gate club for a further seven seasons.

The tricky outside-left created a number of goalscoring opportunities for the likes of John Ateyo and Arnold Rodgers but in 1953-54 when he became the club's penalty-taker, he had his best season in terms of goals scored when he netted 14. The following season he scored 11 times as the Robins won the Third Division (South) Championship but in December 1956 he left to play for Coventry City in the double transfer involving Jimmy Rogers.

He scored 17 goals in 90 games for the Highfield Road club before returning to play for City at the start of the 1960-61 season. He wrote himself into the club's record books when he scored City's first-ever League Cup goal in the 1-1 draw with Aldershot. Boxley had scored 36 goals in 218 games for the Robins when he left to play non-League football for Chippenham Town. He later played for Welton Rovers and Bath City before hanging up his boots.

BRADSHAW, JOE

As a player, winger Joe Bradshaw made little impact at both Fulham and Chelsea but helped Southend United regain their place in the First Division of the Southern League. Bradshaw was player-manager at Roots Hall until the outbreak of the First World War but then left to join the army. On his demob he was appointed manager of Swansea and almost immediately piloted the Swans into the Football League. In 1924-25 he guided the Welsh club to the Third Division (South) Championship and the following season the club won through to the semi-finals of the FA Cup where they lost to Bolton Wanderers at White Hart Lane.

He left Vetch Field in May 1926 to manage Fulham but had a difficult time at Craven Cottage. The London club were relegated for the first time in their history in 1928 and though they scored 101 goals in 1928-29 and finished fifth in the Third Division (South), Bradshaw lost his job.

He then took charge at Bristol City but at the end of his first season at Ashton Gate, the club just managed to avoid the drop by a tenth of a goal ! In 1930-31 City relied on a late run to avoid relegation but in February 1932 after the club had won just three of 32 matches, Bradshaw was sacked with the Robins in a desperate financial position.

BRIDGE, CYRIL

Left-back Cyril Bridge was playing for St Philip's Marsh Adult School in the Bristol and District League when City manager Joe Bradshaw secured his services in the summer of 1930. He spent two seasons in the club's reserve side when eventually in November 1932 his impressive displays were rewarded with a first team debut against Crystal Palace, a match that ended all-square at 3-3. Though he never scored a goal for City, Bridge was a first team regular for five seasons up to the outbreak of the Second World War.

He was an important member of the side that reached the fifth round of the 1934-35 FA Cup competition and just missed out on promotion to the Second Division in 1937-38.

He had appeared in 170 League and Cup games when he decided to hang up his boots. On his death in January 1988, his ashes were scattered on the pitch at Ashton Gate.

BRIGGS, ALEC

Long-serving full-back Alec Briggs was discovered playing football for local club Soundwell when Pat Beasley signed him in April 1957. He made his debut the following season in a 3-2 win at Cardiff City but it was 1961-62 before he won a regular place in the side. Having made just 17 league appearances over the previous four seasons, Briggs was ever-present in 1961-2 as the Robins finished sixth in the Third Division (South). He was ever-present again the following season and again in 1966-67.

Noted for his partnership with Mike Thresher, Briggs helped the club win promotion to the Second Division in 1964-65 and three seasons later, scored his only league goal for the Robins in a 3-1 defeat at Derby County.

He went on to play in 403 first team games for City before leaving Ashton Gate to concentrate on his clothing business.

BRINTON, ERNIE

Left-half Ernie Brinton played his early football with Avonmouth in the Bristol Suburban League and had represented the Gloucestershire FA when City signed him in February 1930. A month later, he made his first team debut in a 1-0 home defeat by Blackpool, going on to play for the Ashton Gate club for the next seven seasons, appearing in 286 League and Cup games, scoring nine goals.

He left Ashton Gate in the summer of 1937 to join Newport County and in his second season at Somerton Park helped the club win the Third Division (South) Championship. During the war years, Brinton 'guested' for City, playing in 109 games. However, when the hostilities were over, he did not return to play for Newport County, he joined Aldershot where he played for one season before bowing out of league football. He then had spells with Street and Chippenham Town in the Western League before hanging up his boots.

BRISTOL ROVERS

The clubs first met in the FA Cup competition of 1901-02. Rovers were leading 2-0 when with just ten minutes to play, the referee abandoned the game because of fog. The second game ended all-square at 1-1 and had gone into extra-time when with just four minutes remaining, the referee brought the match to an early conclusion due to fading light. In the third meeting, Rovers ran out winners 3-2.

The two clubs first played each other in the Football League on 23 September 1922 when Rovers won 1-0 at Ashton Gate. City gained revenge in the return match winning 2-1 with goals from Fairclough and Poulton.

When the Robins won the Third Division (South) Championship in 1926-27 they completed their first 'double' over their rivals, winning 3-1 at home and 5-0 at Eastville with leading goalscorer 'Tot' Walsh netting twice. In 1933-

34, City lost both matches, 3-0 at Ashton Gate and 5-1 at Eastville, their biggest defeat in these meetings.

In 1945-46, the clubs met over two legs in the second round of the FA Cup, City winning 4-2 at home and 2-0 at Eastville. When league football resumed in 1946-47, City won both games and did so again the following season when Don Clark scored a hat-trick in the 5-2 home win over Rovers. In 1952-53 both games ended goalless as they did some 28 years later. One of the highest scoring games between the two clubs occurred in 1956-57 when City won 5-3 in front of an Ashton Gate crowd of 36,981. There was another high-scoring encounter the following season when Rovers beat City 4-3 in the fifth round of the FA Cup. In fact the two league meetings that season had produced 11 goals - City winning 3-2 at home and drawing 3-3 at Eastville. City did the 'double' over Rovers again in 1962-63, a feat they did not repeat again until 1997-98.

The clubs' only meeting in the League Cup came in 1991-92 when City won 3-1 at Twerton Park but lost 4-2 at home, Rovers going through on the away goals rule.

The clubs last met on 22 April 2000 when Rovers won 2-0.

Below are City's statistics against Bristol Rovers:

	P.	W.	D.	L.	F.	A.
Football League	86	33	29	24	122	101
FA Cup	8	4	2	2	15	11
Football League Cup	2	1	0	1	5	5
Freight Rover Trophy	1	1	0	0	3	0
Sherpa Van Trophy	1	0	0	1	0	1
Anglo-Scottish Cup	2	2	0	0	9	2
TOTAL	100	41	31	28	154	120

BROTHERS

There have been a number of instances of brothers playing for Bristol City.

Goalkeeper Frank Vallis who replaced the legendary Harry Clay and went on to make 243 first team appearances was later joined at Ashton Gate by his brothers Gilbert and Henry. Though all three never appeared together in the same City side, Frank and Gilbert appeared in six games together in 1919-20.

Ernie Brinton, a stylish left-half who appeared in 286 games for City, played alongside his younger brother Jack on nine occasions during the 1935-36 and 1936-37 seasons.

Tom Ritchie who was the club's leading goalscorer in five successive campaigns, helping the Robins win promotion in 1975-76 and the Anglo-Scottish Cup in 1977-78, scored 132 goals in 504 games. His younger brother Steve made just one appearance for the club at left-back when Tom was at right-half in a 5-1 defeat at Fulham!

BRYANT, MATT

Bristol-born defender Matt Bryant joined the Ashton Gate club as a trainee before signing professional forms in the summer of 1989. Unable to break into the Robins' first team, he went on loan to Walsall and made his league debut for the Saddlers on the opening day of the 1990-91 season.

On his return to Ashton Gate he had to wait until January 1991 before making his league debut for City in a 1-0 defeat at Plymouth Argyle. He kept his place in the side for the remainder of that season, playing alongside Welsh international Mark Aizlewood. Bryant was a first team regular for the next six seasons, missing very few games and in 1994-95 was voted Player of the Year.

He had scored seven goals in 224 League and Cup games when in July 1996 he joined Gillingham for £65,000.

In his first season at the Priestfield Stadium, he was forced to miss a couple of games due to shooting himself in the leg on a shooting expedition in Bristol! Since then injuries and a loss of form have restricted his appearances to 111 since his move from City.

BURDEN, TOMMY

Wing-half Tommy Burden played for Somerset County Boys and was recommended to Wolves then managed by Major Frank Buckley, by his headmaster. He was only 16 when he played for Wolves in wartime football. He served with the Rifle Brigade and Royal Fusiliers and despite being wounded in the D-Day landings, completed a Physical Education course at Loughborough College. Burden was with Chester when Major Buckley now Leeds' boss, signed him again in July 1948.

Though he continued to live in his beloved West Country, his commitment to the Elland Road club could never be questioned. Appointed Leeds' captain, he stayed with United for just over six years, scoring 13 goals in 259 League and Cup games. He finally asked to move nearer to his Glastonbury home and joined Bristol City in October 1954 for a fee of £1,500 plus £500 a year for three years.

He made his City debut in a 2-0 defeat at Northampton Town but was then switched from wing-half to inside-forward, scoring eight goals in 27 games as the Ashton Gate club won the Third Division (South) Championship. Burden went on to be a first team regular with the Robins for six seasons, scoring 21 goals in 249 games. On leaving Ashton Gate, he had a brief spell playing non-League football for Glastonbury before later working as a senior executive with Clark's shoes in Street, Somerset.

BURTON, ANDY

Inside-left Andy Burton had played his early football for Thompson Rovers and Lochgelly Juniors before joining Motherwell from where Bristol City manager Harry Thickett signed him in 1905.

After making his debut in a 5-1 defeat at Manchester United on the opening day of the 1905-06 season, his next 24 appearances in a City shirt during that campaign saw the club win 20 and draw four of those games as they went on to win the Second Division Championship. The following year Burton collected a League Championship runners-up medal, having his most successful season in terms of goals scored with 13 in 34 league games. In 1909 he was a member of the City side that lost 1-0 to Manchester United in the FA Cup Final at the Crystal Palace. However, two seasons later City were relegated to the Second Division and Burton left Ashton Gate to join Everton. He had scored 51 goals in 216 games for City and had been an influential member of Harry Thickett's side.

He had just one season at Goodison Park, scoring four goals in 12 games before moving to Reading in the Southern League and later coaching in Belgium.

BUSH, TERRY

A versatile player, Terry Bush turned out for City at wing-half and in most of the forward positions. After joining the Ashton Gate club as a junior, he worked his way through the ranks before making his league debut at home to Torquay United in March 1961, a match in which he scored both the Robins' goals in a

2-2 draw. However, it was another four seasons before the Norfolk-born player won a regular place in the City side. In that 1964-65 season, Bush scored 16 goals in 37 games to help the club win promotion to the Second Division. He continued to play for the first team until the summer of 1970 when a knee injury forced him to quit the game prematurely.

Bush, who had scored 46 goals in 185 first team outings, remained at Ashton Gate as the club's assistant-secretary. He later worked as the Manager of the Dolman Stand Indoor Bowling Club before being involved with the Transport and General Workers' Union, initially in Bristol and latterly in Newport.

C

CAIE, ALEX

Alex Caie began his career playing for Victoria United in his home-town of Aberdeen. However, it wasn't long before clubs south of the border began to take an interest in him and in 1896 he joined Woolwich Arsenal. After playing in eight Second Division games for the Gunners in 1896-97 he followed Sam Hollis to Bristol City and made his debut in the club's first-ever Southern League game against Wolverton. Caie scored a hat-trick that day in a 7-4 win and ended the season as the club's top-scorer. His total of 18 goals in 21 games included another hat-trick as Sheppey United were beaten 7-0. Caie continued his goalscoring exploits for the next two seasons but in 1900 after scoring 59 goals in 105 games for the Robins, he left to join Millwall.

A year later he moved to Newcastle United, playing 31 times for the Magpies in the First Division before leaving to join Brentford. He later had a spell with Motherwell before deciding to emigrate to Canada. After playing for the Westmount club, he joined the Sons of Scotland, for whom he was still playing when he was killed on the railway in Massachusetts in December 1914.

CAMPBELL, BOB

Bob Campbell replaced Tom Watson as Sunderland's secretary-manager in August 1896 but after a disappointing season in which the club finished next but one to the bottom of the First Division, they had to take part in a series of Test Matches to decide which teams would play in which division the following season. Campbell piloted the club through these Test Matches to retain their First Division status. The following season, Campbell led the Wearsiders to runners-up in the League Championship, five points behind Sheffield United. After one more season he left to take charge at Bristol City, winning the job from more than 30 applicants. His brief was to mould a team from the players acquired by the committee and he had no secretarial duties. However, despite the club being elected to the Football League under his managership, he left Ashton Gate after a disagreement with the directors over a huge wage bill.

Campbell later managed Bradford City before becoming a member of the Southern League Management Committee and the Referees' Selection Committee.

CAPACITY
The capacity of Ashton Gate in 2000-2001 was 21,479.

CAPTAINS
Bristol City's first captain was centre-half Sandy Higgins. Signed from Grimsby Town, he spent just one season with the Robins, leading them to runners-up in their first season in the Southern League. Billy Wedlock who won 26 caps for England, skippered the Robins to the Second Division Championship in 1905-06 and to runners-up in the First Division the following season, not to mention the FA Cup Final in 1909.

When City won the Third Division (South) Championship in 1922-23 they were skippered by Laurie Banfield and when they repeated the achievement four seasons later, Walter Wadsworth, the former Liverpool player was captain. Jack White was Bristol City's captain when they won the Third Division (South) title again in 1954-55, playing in every game. Scottish wing-half Gordon Low captained the club when they won promotion to the Second Division in 1964-65 whilst Geoff Merrick led the side when they won promotion to the top flight in 1975-76.

When the Robins won through to the Freight Rover Trophy Final at Wembley, it was Bobby Hutchinson who captained the club to a 3-0 win. Versatile defender Rob Newman skippered Bristol City's 1989-90 promotion success whilst Shaun Taylor captained City to promotion to the First Division in 1997-98, leading by example as he has done throughout his long career.

CAREY, LOUIS
Bristol-born Louis Carey graduated from City's School of Excellence to sign professional forms for the club. He made his debut in a 1-0 win at York City in October 1995 and since then has missed very few games.

After playing most of his early football for the club at right-back or wing-half, he seemed to have found his best position in 1997-98 when he played in a sweeper's role alongside Shaun Taylor. Carey's form was such that in consequence of family links, he was rewarded with an appearance for the Scottish Under-21 side in a friendly match against Denmark. He later turned down the chance of a second appearance in the hope that one day England offer him the same opportunity.

After helping the club win promotion in 1997-98, he found life in the higher grade of football a little more difficult but always gave of his best. Still to score his first goal for the club, Carey has now appeared in 195 games for the Ashton Gate club where it is felt, his best days have still to come.

CARNELLY, ALBERT

Much-travelled goalscorer Albert Carnelly began his career with Notts County before later playing for Loughborough, Nottingham Forest and Leicester Fosse. He joined Bristol City, along with Harry Davy for their first Southern League season and their first under that name. He scored twice on his debut in a 7-4 win over Wolverton and ended his first season with the club with 22 goals in 30 league games including four goals in the 6-1 defeat of Chatham. Carnelly also netted four goals in the 9-1 win over Clifton in that season's FA Cup competition. He stayed for one more season with the Robins taking his total of goals to 45 in 63 first team outings.

On leaving City he joined Thames Ironworks (later to become West Ham United) where he twice scored four goals, to repeat the feat he had achieved earlier with the Robins. On leaving the Irons he ended his playing career with Millwall Athletic.

CASEY, TOMMY

Tough-tackling wing-half Tommy Casey began his career with Bangor in his native Northern Ireland. He joined Leeds United in May 1949 but after being unable to win a regular place in the Elland Road club's side, he moved to Bournemouth a year later. His impressive performances for the Cherries led to Newcastle United paying £7,000 for his services in the summer of 1952. With Newcastle he won the first of 12 full caps and played in their 1955 FA Cup winning side. In July 1958, just after he had played in the World Cup Finals for Northern Ireland, he joined Portsmouth and then in March 1959 he signed for Bristol City.

His first game for the Robins was the local derby against Bristol Rovers at Ashton Gate which ended in a 1-1 draw. He was a first team regular with City for three seasons but in July 1963 after scoring nine goals in 133 League and Cup games, he left to become player-manager of Gloucester City.

After a spell as Swansea Town's trainer, he returned to Northern Ireland to manage Distillery. He later coached Everton and Coventry City before managing Grimsby Town who sacked him the day he moved into his newly-purchased house!

CASHLEY, RAY

Goalkeeper Ray Cashley was a left-back when he joined Bristol City but was forced into playing in goal during the club's FA Youth Cup run in 1969-70. He was such a success in his new position that the Ashton Gate club signed him on professional forms the following summer. He made his first team debut for the Robins in a 3-0 defeat at Southampton in an FA Cup third round match in January 1971. After that, Cashley was the club's first-choice 'keeper and in the 3-1 win over Hull City on 18 September 1973, scored one of the goals from a long clearance!

Cashley, who was ever-present in season's 19974-75 and 1975-76, appeared in 109 consecutive league games during which time he helped the club win promotion to the First Division, keeping 19 clean sheets in 42 Second Division games.

However, once in the top flight he seemed to lose form and was displaced by John Shaw. Over the next five seasons, he made only a further 44 league appearances to take his total of League and Cup appearances for the Ashton Gate club to 248.

Cashley, who also had a loan spell with Hereford United, retired before being enticed back to the game by Bristol Rovers. He made 53 league appearances for the Pirates before having spells with Chester City and Bury on loan.

In 1986-87 he returned to Ashton Gate as cover for Keith Waugh but was not called upon.

CENTURIES

There are four instances of individual players who have scored 100 or more league goals for Bristol City. John Ateyo is the greatest goalscorer with 315

Ray Cashley

strikes in his Ashton Gate career (1951-1966). Other centurions are Arnold Rodgers (106) Jimmy Rogers (102) and Tom Ritchie (102).

Mike Gibson holds the club record for the most consecutive league appearances - 177. Other players to have made over 100 consecutive appearances during their careers with the Ashton Gate club are Rob Newman (147) Brian Clark (146) Harry Clay (136) Gordon Low (136) Brian Drysdale (131) Gerry Sweeney (130) John Shaw (124) Alec Briggs (119) and Ray Cashley (109).

CHAMBERS, PETER

Peter Chambers played his early football with Black Diamonds in his native Workington, helping the club win the Cumberland League and Cup.

In 1897 he joined Blackburn Rovers but two years and 33 appearances later, he moved south to join Bedminster. After just one season the club merged with Bristol City and Chambers, who starred as the Robins were runners-up in the Southern League, went on to be a first team regular for the next six seasons. He was a member of the City side that won 2-0 at Blackpool in their first Football League game and in 1905-06 helped the club win the Second Division Championship. He had scored 10 goals in 230 games for City when in the summer of 1907 he was allowed to join Swindon Town.

After helping the Wiltshire club to finish runners-up in two consecutive seasons of Southern League football, he was instrumental in Town winning the Championship in 1910-11. On hanging up his boots, Chambers became landlord of the Red Lion pub in Swindon.

CHAMPIONSHIPS

Bristol City have won a divisional championship on four occasions. In 1905-06 the club won the Second Division Championship though the first match of the season which City lost 5-1 at Manchester United, gave no hint of the success that was to follow. The Robins then won their next 14 matches to equal the run set by Manchester United the previous season and in fact, were unbeaten in 24 matches, next losing 2-1 against Leicester Fosse on 17 February 1906. They were the only defeats of a season which saw City become the first club to win thirty league games in a campaign in which they also created a new points record.

City won the Third Division (South) Championship in 1922-23 after going to the top of the table in mid-December. During the course of the season, City embarked on a 15-match unbeaten run and finished the campaign six points ahead of runners-up Plymouth Argyle.

City's third Championship success came in 1926-27 when the club again won the Third Division (South) Championship following their relegation after just one season of Second Division football. The campaign saw the club establish a number of new records - they beat Gillingham 9-4 with 'Tot' Walsh scoring six times and netted a total of 104 goals - as well as setting a new points record for the division with 62.

The club's fourth Championship was won in 1954-55 when the Robins began the season with a 13-match unbeaten run. They equalled the division's record for both wins (30) and points (70) set by Nottingham Forest four years previously to finish nine points clear of runners-up Leyton Orient.

CHEESLEY, PAUL

Paul Cheesley began his Football League career with Norwich City, appearing in the First Division for the Canaries. However, he was unable to hold down a regular first team place at Carrow Road and in December 1973, he joined Bristol City for a fee of £30,000.

He made his debut for City in a 2-0 home defeat at the hands of Orient on New Year's Day 1974, though it was 1975-76 before he established himself full in the Robins' side. Forming an effective strike force with Tom Ritchie, he scored 15 goals in 38 games as City won promotion to the First Division. Included in his total was a hat-trick in a 4-1 win at York City. Cheesley scored the club's first goal in the top flight as City won 1-0 at Arsenal on the opening day of the 1976-77 season. Unfortunately a knee injury in the 1-1 draw against Stoke City three days later effectively ended his first-class career.

Cheesley, who had scored 21 goals in 70 games, later played non-League football for a number of clubs including Shepton Mallet, Frome Town and Yeovil Town.

CLARK, BRIAN

The son of former Bristol City favourite Don Clark, he joined the Ashton Gate club in March 1960 and made his first team debut in the final game of the 1960-61 season against Brentford, a match City won 3-0 thanks to a John Atyeo hat-trick. After a handful of appearances the following season, Clark came into his own in 1962-63, topping the club's goalscoring charts with 23 goals in 42 games.

Included in that total were hat-tricks in the wins over Watford (Away 4-1) and Hull City (Home 3-1). He continued to find the net on a regular basis and in 1964-65 when the club won promotion to the Second Division, he top-scored again with 24 goals. His total included 12 in the first eight games of the season with hat-tricks against Barnsley (Home 5-1) and Workington Town (Home 5-0). Clark's last hat-trick for the club came in December 1965 as City beat Leyton Orient 4-0 at Brisbane Road. Early the following season, after scoring 93 goals in 220 games he left Ashton Gate to join Huddersfield Town in exchange for John Quigley.

Unable to settle at the Yorkshire club he was snapped up by Cardiff City manager Jimmy Scoular for the bargain fee of £8,000.

He scored twice on his debut for the Bluebirds in a 4-3 win at Derby County and after forming a formidable partnership with John Toshack, netted 17 league goals in 1968–9 and won the first of three Welsh Cup winners' medals. Clark, who topped the Welsh club's scoring charts for three successive seasons, scored the goal that defeated Real Madrid 1-0 in the European Cup Winners' Cup quarter-final first leg to ensure his place in the history of the club. Surprisingly, he and Ian Gibson were allowed to join Bournemouth for a combined fee of £100,000. After twelve months at Dean Court, he joined Millwall before returning to play for the Bluebirds. In 1975-76 he helped the club win promotion to the Second Division but after scoring 108 goals in his two spells, he left to end his league career with Newport County.

On leaving the first-class game, he had spells as player-manager of Maesteg, AFC Cardiff and Bridgend Town.

CLARK, DON

Don Clark's total of 36 league goals in 1946-47 still stands as the most in a season by a Bristol City player. He made his debut for the Robins in a 2-0 home win over Mansfield Town in March 1939 but his career was interrupted by the Second World War. During the hostilities, Clark appeared in 170 wartime games, scoring 63 goals.

When league football resumed, Clark lined-up at centre-forward in the Bristol City side. He had an outstanding season in 1946-47, his 36 goals making him the Third Division (South)'s leading scorer. His total included four goals in the wins over Aldershot (Home 9-0) and Torquay United (Home 5-0) and hat-tricks in the defeats of Exeter City (Away 3-1) and Mansfield Town (Home 5-2). The following season, Clark formed a prolific goalscoring partnership with

Len Townsend, his total of 22 goals including four goals in the 7-2 win over Reading at Elm Park and a hat-trick in the 5-2 defeat of rivals Bristol Rovers.

He had scored 82 goals in 136 League and Cup games when he suffered a serious knee injury against Leyton Orient in February 1949. Though he tried to make a comeback, it was to no avail and in 1951 he was appointed City's assistant-secretary, a position he held for five years.

CLAY, HARRY

Goalkeeper Harry Clay joined Bristol City from Kimberley St John's midway through the 1901-02 season and made his debut in a 5-2 home win over Chesterfield. Ever-present in three successive seasons, he appeared in 136 consecutive league games before injury forced him to miss the game against Manchester United in December 1905.

Clay was the club's first-choice goalkeeper until the 1912-13 season when after appearing in 332 League and Cup games, he gave way to Tommy Ware.

During his 13 seasons with the club, he helped them win the Second Division Championship in 1905-06, keeping 18 clean sheets and reach the FA Cup Final in 1909. He did return to Ashton Gate to play in two wartime games, after which he was head groundsman at the BAC Ground.

CLEAN SHEETS

This is the colloquial expression used to describe a goalkeeper's performance when he does not concede a goal. Frank Vallis had 24 clean sheets from 42 league appearances in 1920-21 when the Robins came third in Division Two.

CLEMENTS, 'HAMMER'

HC 'Hammer' Clements played for both Bedminster and Bristol South End clubs. It was his impressive performances for Redcliffe Boys in Bedminster Park that prompted the Bedminster club to sign him and he made his debut for them at inside-forward in 1893-94. Also able to play at wing-half, 'Hammer' Clements was one of the leading amateur players in the district, a status he maintained throughout his playing career. Clements, who had represented Gloucestershire on a number of occasions also managed to appear in one Southern League game for the Ashton Gate club after they had turned professional as they won 2-1 at New Brompton.

COGGINS, BILLY

Goalkeeper Billy Coggins replaced Frank Vallis in the City side, making his league debut in a 2-1 win at Southend United on Boxing Day 1925. After that, he was the club's first-choice 'keeper for the next five seasons, being ever-present in 1926-27 when the Robins won the Third Division (South) Championship. Coggins who kept 15 clean sheets in that campaign, played in 77 consecutive league games following his debut before injury forced him to miss the match at Swansea in November 1927. He had played in 182 games for the Robins when in April 1930 he was transferred to Everton for £2,000.

He made his debut for the Blues in a 4-2 home defeat by Grimsby Town, a result which condemned the club to relegation from the First Division. In 1930-31, Coggins was an ever-present as Everton raced away with the Second Division Championship. The following season he lost his place to Ted Sagar and unhappy with reserve team football, he left to play for Queen's Park Rangers and later Bath City.

COLE, ANDY

Andy Cole joined Arsenal as a 14-year-old schoolboy in October 1985 before attending the FA School of Excellence at Lilleshall. On his return to Highbury, Cole, who was already a schoolboy international, represented the England Youth side before making his one and only league appearance for the Gunners against Sheffield United in December 1990. With the likes of Smith, Wright, Campbell and Merson ahead of him for selection, he was given two loan spell opportunities at Fulham and Bristol City.

Cole finally left Highbury in July 1992 when City manager Dennis Smith paid £500,000 to bring him to Ashton Gate. His self-confidence in his own ability with his powerful running and his unbelievable awareness in front of goal, stood him in good stead and in eight months at Ashton Gate, he scored 24 goals in 45 games including a hat-trick in a 5-1 League Cup win over Cardiff City.

Newcastle United paid £1.75 million for him in March 1993 and by the end of that season, he had helped the Magpies win the First Division Championship. In 1993-94 he became Newcastle's record goalscorer in a season with 41 goals and was voted the PFA Young Player of the Year. However, in January 1995 he was surprisingly sold to Manchester United for £7 million, a new English transfer record. Later on that season he won the first of

12 full caps for England, whilst with United he has won the European Cup, three Premier League Championship medals and two FA Cup winners' medals. Forming a deadly striking partnership with Dwight Yorke, Cole has now scored 103 goals in 229 first team games for the Red Devils.

Andy Cole

COLLIER, GARY

Bristol-born central defender Gary Collier joined the Ashton Gate club as an apprentice before turning professional in November 1972. After impressing in the club's reserve side, manager Alan Dicks gave him his league debut at Luton Town in March 1973, a match the Robins won 3-1. He made two more appearances at the end of that season, City beating Preston North End 3-1 and Hull City 2-1, both games being played at Ashton Gate.

The following season he won a regular place at the heart of the City defence, his performances alongside Geoff Merrick going a long way in helping the club reach the sixth round of the FA Cup. In 1974-75, Collier missed just one game - a goalless draw at Nottingham Forest on the opening day of the season - a campaign in which he was voted the club's Player of the Year.

In 1975-76, Collier was again in outstanding form as City won promotion to the First Division and was one of two ever-presents the following season, the club's first in the top flight. A series of injuries restricted his first team appearances over the next couple of seasons and in July 1979 after scoring three goals in 215 League and Cup games, he joined Coventry City for a record £325,000.

Unable to win a regular place at Highfield Road, he left to join Portland Timbers for £365,000 just eight months after leaving Ashton Gate. Later playing for San Diego Sockers, Collier has now settled in Florida where he has coached a number of teams.

COLOURS

As Bristol South End, they played in red shirts and navy blue shorts but following the amalgamation with Bedminster to become Bristol City, the players wore red shirts and white shorts, a combination almost unchanged for over 100 years. One of City's few alternatives to a plain red shirt was the double pin-stripe version of 1988 but the club soon returned to its original colours. Bristol City's present colours are red shirts, red shorts and white stockings whilst their change colours are white shirts, white shorts and white stockings.

CONNOR, JACK

Centre-half Jack Connor began his career with Huddersfield Town, playing for the Terriers in their First Division days. Whilst at Leeds Road, Connor had also played at wing-half and centre-forward and had scored 10 goals in 85 league games when City manager Fred Ford brought him to Ashton Gate in October 1960 in exchange for Johnny McCann.

Connor made his City debut in a 2-0 home win over Coventry City and over the next few seasons, missed very few games, being ever-present in 1961-62, 1966-67 and 1968-69. Along with Gordon Low, he helped form an outstanding central defensive partnership and in 1964-65 was instrumental in the club winning promotion to the Second Division.

He went on to score 12 goals in 414 first team outings before being appointed onto City's coaching staff in 1971. He later held a similar position with Everton before deciding to return to the playing side with non-League Fleetwood Hesketh. Connor, who spent 18 years as Area manager for Package Control Ltd, is now back with the sport he loves, as a groundsman at the Everton School of Excellence.

CONSECUTIVE HOME GAMES

Bristol City played an extraordinary sequence of five home games in succession in 63 days during the 1962-63 season in which many games were postponed, with the following results:

Date	Opponents	Competition	Result
22.12.1962	Shrewsbury Town	Third Division	Won 3-1
26.12.1962	Brighton H.A.	Third Division	Lost 1-2
16.01.1963	Aston Villa	FA Cup Round 3	Drew 1-1
16.02.1963	Bradford	Third Division	Won 4-2
23.02.1963	Carlisle United	Third Division	Drew 2-2

CONSECUTIVE SCORING - LONGEST SEQUENCE

Willie Maxwell holds the club record for consecutive scoring when he was on target in nine consecutive league games. His first came in the 2-1 home win over Hull City on 21 October 1905 and ended with a hat-trick in a 4-0 win over Burton United at Ashton Gate on 16 December 1905.

COOK, TONY

Goalkeeper Tony Cook began his career with Clifton St Vincents in the Bristol Downs League. Signed by Bob Wright, he made his league debut for the Robins against Swindon Town in November 1952, saving a penalty in a 4-2 win. In fact, he became renowned for his penalty saves in his 12 seasons at Ashton Gate. During the club's Third Division (South) Championship-winning season of 1954-55, Cook was forced to miss the run-in after breaking his arm against Gillingham. After that, he contested the goalkeeper's jersey with Bob Anderson before regaining the number one spot on a permanent basis in 1958-59. That season, he saved six out of the nine penalties he faced and in the 3-3 draw at Scunthorpe United, he saved Jack Brownsword's penalty twice before Donnelly netted at the third attempt. Ever-present in 1959-60, he missed very few games until he broke his arm for a second time in the match against Queen's Park Rangers midway through the 1962-63 season. Unable to oust Mike Gibson, Cook, who had played in 346 League and Cup games, left Ashton Gate on a free transfer to join Worcester City.

Two years later he moved to Cinderford Town before returning to play Downs League football.

COOPER, TERRY

Terry Cooper won a reputation as a fine attacking left-back with Leeds United. Though his goals were relatively rare, he scored against Arsenal in the 1968 League Cup Final to give the Elland Road club their first major trophy. Two years later he won the first of 20 full caps for England and played in the 1970 World Cup. Cooper went on to make 350 appearances for Leeds before joining Middlesbrough in March 1975.

In July 1978, Alan Dicks paid £20,000 for his services and on being re-united with Norman Hunter, made his City debut in a 2-1 win at Bolton Wanderers on the opening day of the 1978-79 season. It wasn't long though before he left to become player-coach at Bristol Rovers where in his first season, the club were relegated and the Main Stand burnt down! Dismissed in 1981, he played briefly for Doncaster Rovers before joining Bristol City as player-manager in May 1982.

He took the Robins to promotion to Division Three and to the Freight Rover Trophy Final in 1986 and 1987. He later joined the board, thus becoming the first player-manager director since Vivian Woodward at the turn of the century. Cooper, whose one goal in 85 appearances came against Halifax Town in a 3-0 win in February 1983 was sacked towards the end of the 1987-88 season.

He then took charge at Exeter City and led the Grecians to the Fourth Division title in 1989-90 before leaving to manage Birmingham City in the summer of 1991. At the end of his first season at St Andrew's, he led the Blues to promotion as runners-up in the Third Division. In January 1994 he rejoined Exeter City as manager but ill-health forced his resignation, though he later returned to the game as a member of Southampton's coaching staff.

Tony Cooper

CORMACK, PETER

Scottish international Peter Cormack began his career with Hibernian where he was top-scorer for the Easter Road club in successive seasons prior to his £80,000 transfer to Nottingham Forest in March 1970. After two years at the City Ground, Cormack joined Liverpool for a fee of £110,000. He went on to make 168 appearances for Liverpool, scoring 26 goals, though surprisingly not adding to his nine full caps he won with Hibernian and Forest. Cormack had begun his career as an old-fashioned inside-forward but as styles changed, he switched to the midfield. Cormack brought pace and thought to the Liverpool team of the early 1970s and featured in the 1972-73 UEFA Cup and 1973-74 FA Cup triumphs as well as two League Championship campaigns. The emergence of Ray Kennedy threatened his position and in November 1976, Bristol City manager Alan Dicks paid £50,000 for his services.

Cormack made his City debut in a 1-0 win at Spurs, his six goals in 20 games helping the club to retain their top flight status. The following season he helped the Robins to win the Anglo-Scottish Cup, scoring the opening goal of the two-legged final at St Mirren. He had scored 16 goals in 75 games for the Ashton Gate club before leaving to rejoin Hibernian on a free transfer in February 1980.

He later spent four years as manager of Partick Thistle before assisting Allan McGraw at Morton.

CRAWFORD, ALAN

Rotherham-born winger Alan Crawford began his Football League career with his home-town team in 1971. He missed very few games in eight seasons at Millmoor and was ever-present in three successive campaigns including 1974-75 when the Millers won promotion to the Third Division. Crawford, who scored 49 goals in 237 league games for Rotherham, had a brief loan spell with Mansfield Town before joining Chesterfield in the summer of 1979.

He helped the Spireites win the Anglo-Scottish Cup in 1980-81 but in August 1982, Bristol City manager Terry Cooper signed the experienced winger on a free transfer.

He made his debut in a 2-1 home win over Hull City on the opening day of the 1982-83 season, a campaign in which his pin-point crosses helped Glyn Riley and Tom Ritchie to score a good number of their goals. In 1983-84, Crawford scored 15 goals in 31 games including a hat-trick in a 5-0 home win over Torquay United. He had scored 28 goals in 103 League and Cup outings when he left to join Exeter City.

He later played non-League football for Bath City before having a spell as the Robins' youth coach.

CRICKETERS

The only Bristol City players who were cricketers of real note were Arthur Milton, Bobby Etheridge, Ron Nicholls and Barry Meyer.

Arthur Milton was England's last dual international, playing against Austria at Wembley in November 1951 whilst on the books of Arsenal. He helped the Gunners win the League Championship in 1952-53, going on to score 21 goals in 84 games before joining Bristol City in February 1955. He had scored three goals in 14 games for the Robins when he decided to retire to concentrate on his cricket career. For Gloucestershire, Milton scored 30,218 runs at 33.65, including 52 centuries. He also holds the county record for most catches in a career with 718. Milton represented England at Test level on six occasions, scoring 104 on his debut against New Zealand at Headingley in 1958.

Bobby Etheridge, who joined the Robins from Gloucester City, scored 51 goals in 297 games for City, being ever-present in 1961-62 when the club finished sixth in Division Three. He was Gloucestershire's reserve wicket-keeper for ten seasons, helping to dismiss 41 batsmen (33 caught 8 stumped) as well as scoring 796 runs at an average of 15.92.

Goalkeeper Ron Nicholls, who made 44 League and Cup appearances for City, also kept goal for Bristol Rovers and Cardiff City. For Gloucestershire, he scored 23,606 runs at 26.17 with a highest score of 217 against Oxford University in 1962, a season in which he scored 2,059 runs. In 1966, his benefit year, he hit a hundred before lunch in the Gillette Cup match against Berkshire.

Barrie Meyer, who scored a hat-trick in a 6-3 win over Southend United on his final appearance for the Robins before leaving to join Hereford United in the summer of 1963, played for Gloucestershire before becoming a famous Test umpire. He scored 5,368 runs at an average of 14.20 and in his role as wicket-keeper, helped dismiss 826 batsmen (707 caught, 119 stumped).

CURLE, KEITH

Keith Curle began his career as an associated schoolboy with Bristol City but then switched his allegiance to Bristol Rovers, first as an apprentice and then as a professional. He scored on his league debut for Rovers but after failing to command a regular place, he was transferred to Torquay United.

Keith Curle

However, after only four months at Plainmoor he left to sign for Bristol City. He made his league debut for the Robins in a 1-1 draw at York City in February 1984. An influential member of the City side that won the Freight Rover Trophy in 1986, he went on to appear in 153 games, his only goal coming against Newport County (Home 3-1) in March 1986. Curle, who had been converted from midfield to the centre of defence left Ashton Gate to join Reading.

His outstanding displays at the heart of the Royals' defence prompted Wimbledon to sign him. He captained the 'Dons' with distinction but in the summer of 1991, Manchester City paid £2.5 million for his services. Curle eventually won full England honours when he came on as a substitute against the CIS in Mexico in April 1902, following it with his full debut in Hungary two weeks later. He captained the Maine Road club during the first Premier League season of 1992-93 before leaving to join Wolves for £650,000 in August 1996. Curle has now appeared in 122 games for the Molineux club, where his organisational skills have been very much in evidence.

D

DAVY, HARRY
Full-back Harry Davy began his career with his home-town club, Padiham before accruing substantial Lancashire League experience with Heywood Central and Blackpool. In fact, the Seasiders were champions in 1894 and runners-up in the seasons before and after. Davy joined Leicester Fosse in April 1895 where he formed an ever-present full-back partnership with George Swift in 1896-97. He had made 56 appearances for Leicester Fosse when he left the club in the close season of 1897 to join former team-mate Albert Carnelly for Bristol City's inaugural Southern League season.

Davy's first appearance in City's colours came in a 7-4 home win over Wolverton on the opening day of the 1897-98 season. His only goal for the club came in a 2-1 win at New Brompton as the Robins went on to end the season as runners-up to Southampton. The club finished runners-up again the following season but at the end of that campaign, Davy, who had appeared in 65 games for the club, was released.

DEAN, ALF
Much-travelled winger Alf Dean began his career with Walsall, later having spells with West Bromwich Albion, Nottingham Forest and Grimsby Town before joining Bristol City. He made his debut on the opening day of the 1902-03 season, scoring the club's first goal in a 2-1 home win over Chesterfield. In fact, Dean went on to score in the first four games of that season, ending the campaign with 10 goals in 25 games as City finished fourth in Division Two. In 1903-04 when the club again finished fourth in the Second Division, Alf Dean was the Robins' joint leading goalscorer with Fred Corbett. Included in his total of 13 goals was a hat-trick in a 6-0 home win over Burnley. Though he continued to provide scoring chances for the likes of Sammy Gilligan and Albert Fisher, he too scored his fair share. He had netted 38 in 102 games for

City when he was allowed to join Swindon Town prior to the 1905-06 promotion-winning season.

He later played for Millwall Athletic, Dundee and Millwall again where he became captain before ending his career with non-League Wellington Town.

DEBUTS

A number of Bristol City players have cause to remember their debuts for the club but for different reasons. Four City players scored hat-tricks on their debuts - Alfie Rowles against Exeter City in 1937-38, Len Townsend against Southend United in 1947-48, John Galley against Huddersfield Town in 1967-68 and Joe Royle against Middlesbrough in 1977-78.

Goalkeeper Tony Cook saved a penalty on his Robins' debut in a 4-2 win over Swindon Town in November 1952 but full-back Trevor Jacobs had the misfortune to score an own goal in his first for the club at Rotherham United in November 1966.

John Pender holds the unenviable record of being the only Bristol City player to be sent-off on his debut for the club at Blackpool in November 1987.

DEFEATS - FEWEST

During the 1905-06 season, Bristol City went through a 38-match programme and suffered only two defeats in winning the Second Division Championship.

DEFEATS - MOST

Bristol City's total of 26 defeats during the 1959–0 season is the worst in the club's history. Not surprisingly they finished bottom of the Second Division and were relegated.

DEFEATS - WORST

Bristol City's record defeat was when Coventry City beat them 9-0 at Highfield Road on 28 April 1934. The club's worst defeat at home came on 29 September 1923 when Derby County beat the Robins.

DEFENSIVE RECORDS

Bristol City's best defensive record was established in 1905-06 when the club won the Second Division Championship. They conceded just 28 goals in that campaign of 38 matches, losing on just two occasions. The club's worst defensive record was in 1959-60 when they let in 97 goals in finishing bottom of Division Two.

DERRICK, JANTZEN

A former England Schoolboy international, winger Jantzen Derrick was the youngest player to turn out for the Ashton Gate club when he made his Bristol City debut against Lincoln City in November 1959 at the age of 16 years and 324 days. He appeared in six games that season, after which he was a regular in the City side until 1970.

Though creating a number of goalscoring opportunities for his team-mates, he too could score goals, his best season being 1962-63 when he found the net 10 times. He helped the club regain their Second Division status in 1964-65 but in the higher grade of football, he appeared to lack the motivation to succeed. A somewhat enigmatic character, he went on loan to Mansfield Town in March 1971 but returned to Ashton Gate to take his total of League and Cup appearances, in which he scored 36 goals to 297 before joining the French League club, Paris St Germain.

He later returned to these shores to play non-League football for Bath City.

DICKS, ALAN

By his own admission, an average player, Alan Dicks made only one appearance for Chelsea during their League Championship winning season of 1954-55 but worked hard and took an interest in all aspects of the game. He was only 23 when he obtained a coaching badge and shortly afterwards his chance came at Coventry City. He was assistant-manager to Jimmy Hill at Highfield Road as the Sky Blues went from the Third to the First Division but left after Hill's resignation and joined Bristol City as their manager.

After four seasons fighting against relegation, Dicks led the Robins to the League Cup semi-finals in 1971 where they lost 3-1 over two legs to Tottenham Hotspur. The club also reached the quarter-finals two years later. In 1975-76 the club won promotion to the First Division for the first time in 65 years after finishing as runners-up to Sunderland. The Robins survived for four years in the top flight and at one point, Dicks became the longest-serving manager in the Football League. Sadly, the club's stint in the First Division almost bankrupted the Robins - too many players on big wages - and Dicks left Ashton Gate shortly after their relegation in 1980.

He then had a break from soccer, working for a promotion company involved in golf and snooker and also became director of a travel agency. After a season in Greek soccer, he returned to the English game as assistant-manager to Ray Lewington at Fulham. In the summer of 1990, they reversed roles but midway through the following season he lost full control of team affairs when Jimmy Hill took on a more active role. He was later sacked after a string of poor results.

Alan Dicks

DISMISSALS

Though a number of players have been sent-off whilst playing for Bristol City, only John Pender received his marching orders whilst making his debut for the club in a 4-2 defeat at Blackpool on 3 November 1987.

DOHERTY, PETER

Peter Doherty was one of the most exciting and innovative footballers of his time and certainly one of the complete footballers of all time.

Surprisingly turned down by Coleraine before joining Glentoran in 1930, Doherty signed for Blackpool in November 1933 for a fee of £1,500. It was some time before he gained a regular place in the Seasiders' team but when he did, he struck a rich partnership with Jimmy Hampson. Having made the first of 16 appearances for Northern Ireland, Doherty left Bloomfield Road in February 1936 to join Manchester City for £10,000. He soon repaid that fee by helping the Maine Road club win the League Championship the following season. During World War Two he 'guested' for Derby County before signing for £6,000 and teaming up with Raich Carter to win the FA Cup in 1946. Shortly afterwards though, he left Derby after a row with the board who refused him permission to run a hotel near the Baseball Ground.

He later joined Huddersfield Town before becoming player-manager of Doncaster Rovers, whom he led to the Third Division (North) title in 1949-50.

Appointed manager of Northern Ireland, he took his country to the quarter-final of the World Cup in 1958, working well with his captain Danny Blanchflower, who took his ideas on to the pitch.

Unfortunately he did not have such a happy time as manager of Bristol City, his spell of just over two years being probably the lowest point of his career. Though City hovered around the promotion places for much of 1958-59, they fell away to finish 11th before a disappointing campaign in 1959-60 saw them relegated to the Third Division (South) - Doherty was sacked with two months of the season to run. He later had spells as joint-manager of Notts County, chief scout of Aston Villa and assistant-manager of both Preston North End and Sunderland before retiring to live near Blackpool.

DRAWS

Bristol City played their greatest number of drawn league matches in seasons 1919-20, 1965-66 and 1982-83 when 17 of their matches ended all-square and their fewest in 1910-11 and 1959-60 when only five of their matches were drawn. The club's highest scoring draw is 4-4, a scoreline in four games - Aston Villa (Away 1907-08) Torquay United (Home 1952-53) Hull City (Away 1963-64) and Wrexham (Home 1977-78).

DRYSDALE, BRIAN

Brian Drysdale began his career with Lincoln City but after just 21 games for the Sincil Bank club, he was released. His home-town club Hartlepool United signed him on a free transfer and his career blossomed under the new managerial partnership of Brian Clough and Peter Taylor. Drysdale helped the north-east club win promotion to the Third Division in 1967-68 but in May 1969 after making 170 appearances for the 'Pool, he joined Bristol City for a fee of £10,000.

After making his debut in a 1-0 home win over Watford on the opening day of the 1969-70 season, Drysdale went on to appear in 131 consecutive league games, being ever-present in his first three seasons at the club. Though the majority of his 323 League and Cup appearances were at left-back, he also turned out on occasions at right-back before leaving Ashton Gate to join Oxford United, this after a short loan spell with Reading.

He later played non-League football for Shepton Mallett, Clevedon Town and Frome Town.

E

EARLY GROUNDS
The club's origins go back to Bristol South End and their first ground was on St John's Lane until their merger with Bedminster in 1900. Then City had an experimental season playing at St John's Lane and Ashton Gate (the home of Bedminster) after which they spent three seasons at St John's Lane before Ashton Gate became the club's permanent home.

EDWARDS, ROB
Welsh international Rob Edwards began his league career with Carlisle United, making his debut a month before he turned professional in April 1990. He had scored five goals in 48 league games for the Cumbrian side when City manager Jimmy Lumsden paid £135,000 for his services in March 1991.

Edwards made his City debut six months later in a 2-1 defeat at Leicester City after which he became an important member of the Robins' side. Instrumental in the club making progress to the fifth round of the FA Cup in 1991-92 and 1993-94, he has since gone on to produce performances that prompted City to sign him nine years ago,

He made the first of his four full appearances for Wales in August 1997 when he came on as a substitute in a 6-4 defeat by Turkey in Istanbul. Unlucky with injury problems, the combative midfielder scored six goals in 250 League and Cup games for the Robins before leaving to play for Preston North End.

EISENTRAGER, ALEC
A German prisoner-of-war, Alec Eisentrager decided to remain in Britain following his release and played non-League football for Trowbridge Town. His goalscoring performances for the Wiltshire club led to Bristol City manager Bob Wright signing him in the summer of 1949.

Eisentrager made his City debut in a 3-1 home win over Northampton

Town on the opening day of the 1949-50 season, whilst in only his fifth game of the campaign, he netted four goals in a 6-0 win over Newport County. He spent nine seasons at Ashton Gate, scoring 47 goals in 240 games with a best of 12 in 1952-53, including a spell of six in successive games.

On leaving Ashton Gate, Eisentrager joined Merthyr Tydfil, later playing for Chelmsford City and Westbury Park.

ELECTION TO FOOTBALL LEAGUE

Despite finishing runners-up in the Southern League for the third time in four seasons, Bristol City were hopeful of Football League membership although they had to compete with clubs seeking re-election to the Second Division. The Robins finished joint-top of the poll at the Football League AGM in Manchester on 17 May 1901 with Burton Swifts who were successful in their bid for re-election. Both clubs collected 23 votes, seven ahead of nearest challengers, Doncaster Rovers.

ELLIOTT, SID

Sunderland-born centre-forward Sid Elliott was playing for Third Division Durham City when Fulham picked him up for a small fee in May 1927. In his only season at Craven Cottage, Elliott was the club's top-scorer with 26 goals including a hat-trick against Bristol City! In May 1928 he joined Chelsea for a record £3,600 and though he helped them regain their top flight status, he was not a great success at Stamford Bridge.

In July 1930, Elliott joined Bristol City and in his first season with the club was the leading goalscorer with 15 goals in 25 games. He stayed for just two seasons at Ashton Gate, scoring 28 goals in 54 League and Cup games before joining Notts County in March 1932. He later played for Bradford City before ending his league career with Rochdale.

EMANUEL, JOHN

Though he made a relatively late start to his football career, joining City from the Ferndale club in Swansea in the summer of 1971, John Emanuel soon made up for lost time. He was 23 years old when he made his league debut for the Robins in a 3-3 home draw against Millwall on the opening day of the 1971-72 season. In only his second season at Ashton Gate, Emanuel was voted the club's Player of the Year, his performances leading to him winning full international honours for Wales at the end of that campaign.

Surprisingly after receiving international recognition, his form took a dip and after losing his place, he had loan spells with Swindon Town and Gillingham.

Emanuel left Ashton Gate in June 1976 to join Newport County, having scored 10 goals in 138 League and Cup games for City. After two seasons at Somerton Park, he had spells with Barry Town and Ton Pentre and is currently the manager of the latter club.

ETHERIDGE, BOBBY

Footballing-cricketer Bobby Etheridge began his career with Gloucester City and after ending the 1954-55 season as the club's leading scorer, was instrumental the following season in their Southern League Cup success.

Bristol City manager Pat Beasley signed him in the summer of 1956 and he made his debut in a 5-1 home win over Lincoln City on 15 December 1956. Etheridge, who was ever-present in 1961-62 was a first team regular at Ashton Gate for seven seasons, though towards the end of his spell with the Robins, he was converted from inside-forward to wing-half. Forming an effective partnership with John Ateyo, his best season for the club in terms of goals scored was 1958-59 when he netted 13 in 41 games. Etheridge, who went on to score 49 goals in 288 League and Cup games later joined Cheltenham Town as player-manager but eventually returned to his roots as manager of Gloucester City.

Etheridge also kept wicket for Gloucestershire for ten years, making 41 dismissals (33 caught and 8 stumped).

EVER-PRESENTS

Fifty-six Bristol City players have been ever-presents throughout a Football League season. The greatest number of ever-present seasons by a City player is four by John Ateyo and Gerry Sweeney. Next in line are Alec Briggs, Brian Clark, Harry Clay, Jack Connor, Brian Drysdale, Mike Gibson, Geoff Merrick, Rob Newman and John Shaw with three each.

F

FA CUP

The club's first match in the FA Cup under the name of Bristol City saw them beat Clifton 9-1 with Carnelly and Wyllie scoring four goals apiece but then after beating Trowbridge Town 5-2, City lost 2-0 at Southampton in the third qualifying round. In 1898-99, City became the first local club to win through to the first round proper but despite a brave showing, they lost 4-2 at home to Sunderland.

In January 1909, City embarked on an FA Cup run that saw them reach the final. They got there the hard way, with replays in every round except the third. After being held to a 1-1 draw at home by Southampton, goals from Hardy and Rippon(penalty) gave the Robins a 2-0 win at the Dell. Round two saw City entertain Bury, a game which ended all-square at 2-2 but in the replay at Gigg Lane, Sammy Gilligan, who had scored City's second goal in the first match, headed home the only goal of the replay. Norwich City were beaten 2-0 in the third round. After a goalless draw at Glossop, another Sammy Gilligan goal was enough to take City into the semi-final where they faced Derby County at Stamford Bridge. Trailing 1-0, they were saved by a last minute penalty by Willis Rippon and it was another Rippon penalty that helped them to a 2-1 win in the replay at St Andrew's four days later. In the final, City, who were without Rippon, injured in a league game, lost 1-0 to Manchester United.

In 1919-20, City beat Grimsby Town, Arsenal, Cardiff City and Bradford City to reach the semi-finals where their opponents at Stamford Bridge were Huddersfield Town. In a fairly even contest, the Yorkshire side won 2-1.

The club's next decent run in the FA Cup was in 1934-35 when they reached the fifth round. After beating Gillingham (Home 2-0) and Rotherham United (Away 2-1), City met Bury in the third round. Following draws at Ashton Gate (1-1) and Gigg Lane (2-2 after extra-time) the clubs met at Villa Park where two goals from Jack Hodge gave the Robins a 2-1 win. The tie against Portsmouth in round four saw the ground attendance record broken as 42,885 saw the sides play out a goalless draw. After winning the replay at Fratton Park, the record gate was again broken as 43,335 crammed into Ashton Gate for the fifth round meeting with Preston North End. Again there were no goals but in the replay at Deepdale, the Lancashire club won 5-0.

In the two seasons following the resumption of league football after the Second World War, City scored nine goals in the FA Cup competition, beating Hayes 9-3 with Don Clark scoring four times and Dartford 9-2 with Clark, Townsend and Williams all netting hat-tricks. In 1960-61, the Robins gained their record FA Cup victory, beating non-League Chichester City 11-0 with John Ateyo scoring five of the goals. Dartford were on the receiving end of another heavy FA Cup defeat in 1961-62 as City won 8-2. Two seasons later, the Robins suffered their worst FA Cup defeat when they lost 6-1 at Sunderland.

In 1973-74, Alan Dicks' Bristol City reached the sixth round of the FA Cup, achieving national fame when a Don Gillies goal helped defeat League leaders and Cup favourite, Leeds United in a replay. Sadly City lost 1-0 at home to Liverpool in the quarter-final at Ashton Gate.

In 1988-89 City were involved in their longest-ever FA Cup tie when the match against Aldershot went to three replays before City won 1-0. Unfortunately they then lost by the same score at Hartlepool in the next round. In recent seasons the club have struggled to make much progress in the competition but in 1996-97 they did beat St Alban's City 9-2 with Paul Agostino scoring four of the goals.

FA CUP FINAL

The club's first and to date, only appearance in an FA Cup Final took place at the Crystal Palace on 24 April 1909 where their opponents were Manchester United. Both clubs had shown their pedigree in the League, with United having won the Championship the year before and City having finished runners-up in 1906-07.

United were pre-match favourites though the Robins had taken three points off them in the League.

A crowd of 71,401 saw the teams take to the field in alternative strips - United sporting their Airdrieonian-style shirt with large red-V and City playing in unfamiliar royal blue. The only goal of a disappointing game was scored by United's Sandy Turnbull in the 22nd minute when he opportunely stabbed the ball into the net after it had rebounded from the crossbar. The City team that day was: H.Clay; A.Annan; J.Cottle; P.Hanlin; B.Wedlock; A.Spear; F.Staniforth; B.Hardy; S.Gilligan; A.Burton and F.Hilton.

FAIRCLOUGH, ALBERT

Albert Fairclough began his league career with Manchester City, following impressive spells for both St Helen's Town and Eccles Borough. Unfortunately the First World War interrupted his career at Maine Road and when League football resumed after the hostilities he joined Southend United.

During the Shrimpers first season in the Football League, 1920-21 Fairclough was the club's leading scorer, a feat that prompted City manager Joe Palmer to pay £2,300 for his services in March 1921. He made his debut in a goalless draw at Birmingham and though he netted five goals in eight appearances, the Robins just failed in their bid to win promotion to the First Division. Despite the club finishing bottom of Division Two the following season, Fairclough was the club's leading scorer. In 1922-23 when the Robins won the Third Division (South) Championship, Fairclough again topped the charts with 22 goals, netting hat-tricks against his former club Southend United (Away 3-0) and in the FA Cup against Wrexham (Home 5-1). He went on to score 47 goals in 94 games before leaving to join Derby County.

After helping the Rams win promotion in 1925-26, his second season at the Baseball Ground, he left to end his career with Gillingham.

FATHER AND SON

Though there have been a number of father and son combinations that have played for Bristol City, the most notable is without doubt, Don and Brian Clark. Don Clark was switched from wing-half to forward during the Second World War and in 1946-47, the first season of League football after the hostilities, he scored 36 goals in 37 games to top the Third Division (South) scoring charts. He went on to score 85 goals in 140 games before a serious knee injury forced his retirement. His son Brian was a much-travelled striker who scored goals wherever he played. Beginning his career with the Ashton Gate club, he was ever-present in three successive seasons and top scorer with 24 goals in the promotion-winning season of 1964-65. He had scored 93 goals in 220 games before leaving to play for Huddersfield Town in an exchange deal involving Johnny Quigley.

Arnold Rodgers, who was City's leading goalscorer in four consecutive seasons, helped the club win the Third Division (South) Championship in 1954-55. He had scored 111 goals in 204 League and Cup games when he left to join Shrewsbury Town. His son David was a central defender of the highest quality, scoring 18 goals in 227 League and Cup games before the 'Ashton Gate Eight' crisis forced his move to Torquay United.

FEAR, KEITH

Former England Schoolboy international Keith Fear made his league debut for Bristol City in a 1-0 defeat at Middlesbrough in October 1970, but despite a number of impressive performances over the next couple of seasons, it was 1972-73 before he won a regular place in the side. Though he wasn't a prolific goalscorer he did score a number of vital goals, perhaps none more so than the equaliser against Leeds United in an FA Cup fifth round game at Ashton Gate in February 1974. That game ended all-square but in the replay at Elland Road, it was Fear who laid on the ball for Don Gillies to score the winning goal.

He helped the club win promotion to the First Division but after just 26 appearances in the top flight in which he scored six goals, he was allowed to leave Ashton Gate. The talented forward who had scored 35 goals in 171 League and Cup games joined Plymouth Argyle following loan spells at Hereford United and Blackburn Rovers.

After two seasons at Home Park in which he scored nine goals in 45 games, he had a brief loan spell with Brentford before ending his first-class career with Chester City.

FESTIVAL OF BRITAIN

In May 1951, the Robins played three games in the Festival of Britain, beating Hambourn 07 1-0, Castle Cary 6-1 and Dinamo FC 2-1.

FIRST DIVISION

Bristol City have had four spells playing in the First Division. Their first began in 1906-07 following their success the previous season in winning the Second Division Championship. In fact, in their first-ever season of top flight football, the Robins almost won the League Championship, finishing as runners-up, three points behind Newcastle United. Only a late run of five undefeated home matches saved the club from relegation in 1907-08 enabling them to finish 10th. After

City had finished eighth in 1908-09 and 16th in 1909-10, the club were relegated the following season after a campaign which saw them score just one goal in their opening seven matches !

The club's second spell in the First Division began in 1976-77 when after a promising start, the campaign turned into a relegation struggle. After four seasons the Robins lost their place in the top flight, finishing 20th in 1979-80, four points adrift from next club Everton.

Following reorganisation, City began their third spell in the 'new' First Division in 1992-93 but after three seasons were relegated. The club returned to Division One in 1997-98 as runners-up to Watford but were relegated after just one season.

FIRST LEAGUE MATCH

Bristol City's first Football League match saw them visit Bloomfield Road to play Blackpool on 7 September 1901. Two goals from inside-forward Paddy O'Brien gave City a 2-0 win. The Bristol City team was: W.Moles; W.Tuft; R.H.Davies; W.Jones; J.McLean; P.Chambers; J.L.Bradbury; M.J.Connor; T.Boucher; P.O'Brien and J.Flynn.

FIRST MATCH

Bristol City were formerly known as Bristol South End and their first match was on 1 September 1894 against Swindon Town who were billed as the 'Champions of the West'. The admission fee was 3d, enclosure 3d extra with no dogs admitted ! For the record, Swindon won 4-2 in front of a crowd of 3,500.

FISHER, ALBERT

After moving south of the border from Celtic, Albert Fisher made just one league appearance for Aston Villa but was top scorer for the Reserves in the Birmingham League. Unable to settle, he joined Fulham and played for the Cottagers in the first Southern League game of 1903-04. After four more appearances in the early qualifying rounds of the FA Cup, Fisher moved to Bristol City, making his debut in a 2-2 draw at Manchester United, when he scored the Robins' second goal.

In 1904-05, Fisher was City's leading goalscorer with 13 goals in 26 games but at the end of the season after which he had taken his tally of goals to 26 in 63 games, he left to play for Brighton and Hove Albion. He later played for

Manchester City and Bradford Park Avenue before switching to non-League soccer in Scotland.

In June 1912 he became secretary-manager of Merthyr Town but before long, he was enticed away to become the first secretary-manager of Notts County. At the end of his first season, the club won promotion to the top flight as Second Division champions. Despite being relegated in 1919-20, Fisher led them to the Second Division title again in 1922-23 but left Meadow Lane at the end of a disappointing 1926-27 campaign when he felt it was time to leave the pressures of club management.

FLOODLIGHTS

The first floodlights at Ashton Gate were designed by the club's chairman Harry Dolman who was an engineer. Mounted on 14 removable poles along each touchline, the lamps which had to be switched on individually, cost £3,500. Primitive by modern-day standards, they were first switched on for a friendly against Wolverhampton Wanderers on 27 January 1953, when a crowd of 23,866 turned up to see the First Division side win 4-2. The first competitive match under the Ashton Gate lights was a Football Combination game against Swansea Town Reserves on 24 February 1953 which the Robins won 2-1. Over the next few years, the lights were used for a number of lucrative friendly matches but in 1965 they were sold to Burton Albion for £2,000. The club then had to find £27,000 for their replacements, four pylons each with 48 lamps. Wolves were again the visitors when the second set of lights were switched on for the Second Division game on 28 December 1965, a match the visitors won 1-0. Later extra lights were fitted in front of the Dolman Stand, whilst the number of lamps on the pylons was gradually reduced.

Following the Taylor Report, new floodlights were installed along the front of both side stand roofs. The existing corner pylons were offered free of charge to any club willing to take them away and in the summer of 1992, Wigan Athletic duly obliged.

FOOTBALL LEAGUE CUP

After receiving a first round bye, the Robins played Aldershot at the Recreation Ground on 10 October 1960 and drew 1-1 with Jack Boxley scoring the club's first-ever goal in the competition. A 3-0 win in the replay proved to be the club's only success in the competition as they went out in the next round 2-1 at Nottingham Forest. The club's next win in the League Cup was on 13 August 1968 when goals from Galley and Garland helped them beat Newport County 2-0. Galley scored the only goal of the game in the next round as Middlesbrough were beaten 1-0 but City then lost 2-1 at Leeds United.

In 1970-71, the Robins reached the semi-finals of the League Cup for the first time. After beating Rotherham United, Blackpool, Leicester City and Fulham, City met Tottenham Hotspur in the two-legged semi-final. In the first match at Ashton Gate, Alan Skirton's goal was cancelled out by Spurs' Scottish international striker, Alan Gilzean. The second leg at White Hart Lane went to extra-time but goals from Chivers and Pearce gave the home side a 2-0 win.

City last progressed to the semi-finals of the League Cup again in 1988-89 with wins over Exeter City, Oxford United, Crystal Palace, Tranmere Rovers and Bradford City. The Robins' opponents in the semi-final were Nottingham Forest. A 1-1 draw at the City Ground with Paul Mardon scoring for the Robins set things up for an interesting second leg at Ashton Gate. Despite being shown live on television, it attracted record receipts from the 28,084 crowd. Unfortunately Forest won 1-0 with the goal coming just six minutes from the end of extra-time.

Since then City haven't progressed further than the second round.

FOOTBALL LEAGUE TROPHY

Formerly known as the Football League Group Cup, it was founded in 1981 as a replacement for the defunct Anglo-Scottish Cup. In 1982-83, Bristol City were one of 32 entrants invited from the Second, Third and Fourth Division clubs who had shown an interest in participating in the competition. The clubs were divided into eight groups off our with the top team from each group playing in a knockout stage later in the season. The Robins beat Torquay United (Home 1-0) but lost to Exeter City (Away 1-2) and Newport County (Home 1-4) and so failed to qualify for the knockout stages.

FORD, FRED

Fred Ford lost most of his playing career to the Second World War but had developed into a footballing centre-half, making 22 appearances for Charlton Athletic, whom he joined in 1935.

During the hostilities, Fred Ford served in the Royal Engineers, losing a finger in a freak accident during his military service. When league football resumed in 1946, he joined Millwall and appeared in nine games before moving to Carlisle United as the Cumbrian club's player-coach. In 1955 he took up a similar post with Bristol Rovers and in his first season at Eastville, almost helped the club win promotion to Division One.

In July 1960, Fred Ford joined Bristol City as manager. The Ashton Gate club had just been relegated to the Third Division but Ford built a team which won promotion in 1964-65 and then the following season were just two victories away from a second successive promotion to the top flight. Unfortunately 1966-67 saw the Robins struggle against relegation and early the following season, Ford was dismissed.

He became coach at Swindon but in April 1968 he returned to Eastville as team-manager. He left Rovers in October 1969 to take over the reins at the County Ground. Whilst with the Wiltshire club he built a reputation as a talent scout, discovering several useful youngsters. He left Swindon in May 1971 and had a spell as coach to Torquay United before being appointed Oxford United's youth coach.

In January 1981 Fred Ford was given a special award for his services to football but died in October of that year.

FORD, TONY

Former England Youth international full-back Tony Ford joined Bristol City as an apprentice before signing professional forms in November 1961. After a series of impressive performances, manager Fred Ford (no relation) gave him his first team debut at Swindon Town in March 1962. In a match in which John Ateyo scored a hat-trick, Ford gave a very polished performance in a 4-0 win. However, over the next three seasons, Ford only made 24 league appearances and it was 1964-65 before he established himself in the City side.

That season, he was ever-present as the Robins won promotion to the Second Division. Volunteering to be the club's penalty-taker, he scored five times from the spot in that campaign and when he did, City ran out winners. Ford was the club's first-choice right-back for the next three seasons but following the emergence of Trevor Jacobs, found his first team opportunities limited.

In December 1969, Ford, who had scored 12 goals in 184 League and Cup games, left Ashton Gate to join Bristol Rovers.

Appointed captain at Eastville, he had made 28 league appearances for the

Pirates when a ruptured spleen ended his playing career. He then coached Plymouth Argyle before assisting John Sillett at Hereford United and Bobby Moncur at Hearts.

FORMATION

The name Bristol City came into being in 1897 when the Bristol South End club, formed some three years earlier, decided to turn professional and apply for admission to the Southern League after playing in the Western League. The historic meeting took place at the Albert Hall, Bedminster. In 1901 the club merged with Bedminster, another leading Bristol club, in which year they joined the Football League as members of the Second Division.

FOURTH DIVISION

Bristol City have had just one spell of two seasons in the Fourth Division following their relegation to the League's basement in 1981-82. After a humiliating 7-1 defeat at Northampton Town, the club plummeted to the foot of the Football League following a 1-0 defeat at Rochdale. Thankfully things improved and City finished the season in 14th place. In 1983-84, City won promotion, finishing fourth behind runaway champions York City, Doncaster Rovers and Reading. The club's total of 82 points was 19 behind the champions.

FREIGHT ROVER TROPHY

The Freight Rover Trophy replaced the initial Associate Members' Cup for the 1984-85 season. That season the Robins beat Hereford United 2-1 on aggregate before two goals from Alan Walsh helped City beat Port Vale 2-1. Walsh was on target from the penalty-spot in the Southern Area quarter-final but City lost 2-1 at home to Newport County.

In 1985-86, the Robins' first group game at home to Plymouth Argyle failed to produce a goal but a 2-1 win at Walsall in the club's second group game took them through to the knockout stages. Goals from Hutchinson, Neville and Riley gave City a 3-2 win over Northampton Town and this was followed by a 3-0 victory over Gillingham to set up a two-legged Southern Area final against Hereford United. After losing 2-0 at Edgar Street in the first leg, City struggled to make much impact in the return meeting at Ashton Gate. A Glyn Riley header gave the Robins hope just after the hour and then in the 64th minute, Bobby Hutchinson brought the aggregate scores level. The game went into extra-time and looked to be heading to a penalty shoot-out when Steve Neville struck in the dying seconds to send the Robins to Wembley for the first time in their history. Their opponents were Bolton Wanderers and having twice beaten the Trotters in the season's league meetings, City were favourites to lift the trophy. Yet it was Bolton who had the better of the opening exchanges with Tony Caldwell rattling Keith Waugh's crossbar. City took the lead in the 44th minute when Glyn Riley fired home following a poor punch out by Bolton 'keeper Simon Farnworth. The second-half was one-way traffic and goals from Pritchard and Riley again gave the Robins a comprehensive 3-0 victory.

City began the defence of the trophy with a 1-1 draw at Exeter City before a 3-0 home win over Bristol Rovers gave them a place in the knockout stage of the competition. After beating Southend United 1-0, two goals from Joe Jordan helped City beat Brentford 3-0 to set up a Southern Area semi-final tie with Gillingham who the Robins beat 2-0. In the two-legged Southern Area final, Joe Jordan scored in both matches as City won through to Wembley again with a 4-1 aggregate victory over Aldershot. In the final which was played on a Sunday in front of a record crowd of 58,586, City fell behind to an early Mansfield goal before Glyn Riley equalised against the run of play in the closing minutes. With no further goals the tie went to a penalty shoot-out which Mansfield won 5-4.

G

GALLEY, JOHN

John Galley began his career with Wolverhampton Wanderers, signing professional forms in May 1961. Unable to hold down a regular place in the Molineux side, he moved to Rotherham United in December 1964. In three years at Millmoor, Galley scored 48 goals in 112 games before leaving to join Bristol City for a fee of £25,000.

Galley made his Robins' debut at Huddersfield Town on 16 December 1967 and scored all the club's goals in a 3-0 win. Replacing Hugh McIlmoyle, Galley scored 16 goals in 21 games in 1967-68, a return which saved the club from relegation to the Third Division.

Galley was the club's leading scorer in four of his five full seasons with the Robins, with a best of 22 in 37 games in 1971-72. This total included another hat-trick in a 5-1 win at Sheffield Wednesday. Galley had scored 91 goals in 195 League and Cup games when he left Ashton Gate in December 1972, joining Nottingham Forest for £30,000.

After a loan spell with Peterborough United, Galley left the City Ground and joined Hereford United. Converted to centre-half by manager John Sillett, he starred in the Edgar Street club's Third Division title success in 1975-76.

He later played non-League football for Telford United and Atherstone Town before hanging up his boots.

GARLAND, CHRIS

Chris Garland had three spells with the Robins, during which time he played in all four divisions of the Football League. Signed as an apprentice in 1966, manager Alan Dicks gave him his league debut in a 2-0 home win over Preston North End in December of that year. The following season he struck up a good understanding with John Galley, his form leading to him winning England Under-23 honours in 1970.

Chris Garland

In September 1971, Chelsea paid £100,000 to take Garland to Stamford Bridge and he appeared for the Blues in their 1972 League Cup Final defeat by Stoke City. Having lost his goalscoring touch, he was allowed to join Leicester City in February 1975 for £95,000. His move had an inspirational effect on the Foxes and his eight goals in ten games at the end of 1974-75 helped the club avoid relegation. He had scored 19 goals in 63 games for the Filbert Street club when they accepted the Robins' offer of £110,000 to bring him home.

His five goals in the last seven games of that 1976-77 season kept the club in the First Division but his second spell with the club was dogged by injuries and indeed his contract was twice cancelled, although one of these was to help the club from the brink of closure. However, he refused to lie down and was still turning out for the Robins on a non-contract basis in 1982-83 to take his tally of League and Cup goals to 50 in 236 appearances.

He later had spells as player-coach of Yeovil Town and player-manager of Minehead before it was revealed that he was suffering from Parkinson's Disease. Bristol City played Manchester United on his behalf in May 1993.

GAVIN, MARK

Mark Gavin started his career with Leeds United where he understudied both Peter Barnes and Frank Gray. After a loan spell at Hartlepool, he was snapped up by Carlisle United but in March 1986, Bolton Wanderers paid £4,000 for his services. He became a regular in the Wanderers team and ended his first season at the club with a Wembley appearance against Bristol City in the Freight Rover Trophy Final. After Bolton had been relegated to the Fourth Division, Gavin moved to Rochdale for a fee of £20,000. After half a season at Spotland, he went north of the border to Hearts but could not force his way into their Premier Division side and in October 1988 he joined Bristol City for £35,000.

He scored on his Robins debut in a 1-0 win at Gillingham and was a first team regular for two seasons, helping the club win promotion to the Second Division in 1989-90. At the end of that campaign he was allowed to join Watford in part-exchange for Wayne Allison. In December 1991, Jimmy Lumsden paid £60,000 to bring him back to Ashton Gate and he went on to score nine goals in 143 League and Cup games in his two spells with the club before joining Exeter City.

Despite being hampered by injuries at St James Park, Gavin appeared in 88 games for the Grecians before joining Scunthorpe United in the summer of 1996 and later ending his career with Hartlepool United.

GIBSON, MIKE

A former England Youth international, goalkeeper Mike Gibson played non-League football for Gresley Rovers and Nuneaton Borough before Shrewsbury Town gave him the chance to play in the Football League in March 1960. After three seasons at Gay Meadow during which time he made 76 Third Division appearances and helped the club reach the League Cup semi-finals, he was sold to Bristol City for £6,000.

He made his City debut in a 1-1 home draw against Crystal Palace at the end of the 1962-63 season, after which he was the club's first-choice 'keeper for the next nine seasons.

He was ever-present in seasons 1964-65, 1965-66 and 1966-67, appearing in 177 consecutive league games. When City won promotion to the Second Division in 1964-65, Gibson kept 15 clean sheets. He helped the club reach the League Cup semi-finals in 1970-71 but midway through the following season he lost his place to Ray Cashley and joined Gillingham at the end of the campaign. He had played in 376 League and Cup games for City and was one of the best goalkeepers ever to play for the club.

After helping Gillingham win promotion to the Third Division in 1973-74, his playing career was ended when he damaged a shoulder. Finding work as a postman, he still assists at Ashton Gate on a part-time basis.

GILLIES, DON

After playing his early football with Inverness Clachnacuddin, Don Gillies joined Morton where he topped the club's scoring charts in each of his two seasons at Cappielow Park. His form not only led to him winning Scottish Under-23 honours but also attracted the attention of a number of clubs south of the border.

Bristol City manager Alan Dicks was the first to react, securing Gillies' services for £30,000 as Steve Ritchie moved in the opposite direction. Gillies made his league debut in a 1-0 defeat at Nottingham Forest in March 1973, appearing in the last 11 games of the season and helping City finish fifth in Division Two.

In 1974-75, Gillies was the club's leading scorer, albeit with just nine goals and the following season when City won promotion to the First Division, most of his 25 league appearances were at right-back. He helped the Robins win the Anglo-Scottish Cup in 1977-78, scoring one of the goals in the semi-final defeat of Hibernian. He had scored 28 goals in 224 League and Cup games before leaving Ashton Gate to follow Terry Cooper to Bristol Rovers for £50,000 in the summer of 1980.

He made 59 appearances for the then Eastville club before playing non-League football for Paulton Rovers, Gloucester City, Bath City and Yeovil Town.

GILLIGAN, SAMMY

Dundee-born centre-forward Sammy Gilligan played his early football with local club Belmont Athletic before joining his home-town team Dundee FC. During his one and a half seasons with the club, the Dark Blues were Scottish League runners-up and Scottish Cup semi-finalists. He moved to Celtic where he won a Scottish Cup winners' medal before Bristol City manager Sam Hollis brought him to Ashton Gate in the summer of 1904.

He scored on his debut on the opening day of the 1904-05 season but City lost 4-3 at home to Bolton Wanderers. Having topped the scoring charts that season, he repeated the feat in 1905-06 as City won the Second Division Championship. His total of 20 goals in 37 games included 13 goals in seven consecutive league games. In two consecutive games in that spell he scored four goals in the wins over Glossop (Away 5-1) and Stockport County (Home 7-0). Forming a good strike partnership with Willie Maxwell, Gilligan was top-scorer for a third time in 1907-08. A member of the City side that lost 1-0 to Manchester United in the FA Cup Final of 1909. Gilligan scored 92 goals in 217 games for City before leaving to play for Liverpool in May 1910.

After three seasons at Anfield in which time he made 41 league appearances, he joined Gillingham as player-manager. During the First World War he played for Dundee Hibernian before ending his career with Forfar Athletic.

GLENN, ERNIE

Redditch-born left-back Ernie Glenn began his career with Willenhall Town where his performances attracted the attention of a number of top clubs. It was Bristol City manager Alex Raisbeck who persuaded the tough-tackling defender to join the Ashton Gate club and he made his debut in a 1-1 home draw against Blackpool in November 1923.

After that, Glenn missed very few games over the next eight seasons and in 1926-27 helped the club win the Third Division (South) Championship. Partnering the likes of Dick Hughes and Jack Walsh, he was one the few players to continue to impress in the higher grade of football.

He had made 288 League and Cup appearances for City when after failing to agree terms, he was placed on the transfer list. Though Robins' fans were hoping things would sort themselves out, they didn't and at the age of 29, Ernie Glenn decided to hang up his boots.

GOALKEEPERS

Bristol City FC has almost always been extremely well served by its goalkeepers and most of them have been highly popular with the supporters.

Harry Clay was one of the club's most famous goalkeepers, helping the Robins win the Second Division Championship in 1905-06 and reach the FA Cup Final in 1908-09. Ever-present in three successive seasons, the long-serving 'keeper appeared in 350 League and Cup games for the club. Frank Vallis kept goal for the club when they reached the FA Cup semi-finals in 1919-20 and won the Third Division (South) Championship three seasons later. Ever-present in the club's first two seasons after the Great War, he went on to appear in 243 first team games. Billy Coggins was ever-present when the Robins won the Third Division (South) Championship for a second time in 1926-27. He had made 182 appearances for the Ashton Gate club before being transferred to Everton. One of the club's most popular 'keepers was Bob Anderson who shared the goalkeeping duties with Tony Cook, saved a penalty on his league debut for the Robins but two season later after making the number one spot his own, broke his arm and was forced to miss the run-in to the Third Division Championship. Cook who played in 355 League and Cup games was at the peak of his career when another broken arm let in probably the club's greatest 'keeper Mike Gibson. The ex-England Youth international was the club's first-choice goalkeeper for eight seasons. Ever-present in three successive seasons, he helped the club win promotion in 1964-65 and reach the League Cup semi-finals in 1970-71. He had made 383 appearances for the Robins when in July 1972 he moved to Gillingham. Ray Cashley switched from playing left-back to goalkeeping during the club's FA Youth Cup run of 1969-70. An ever-present for City when they won promotion in 1975-76, he found the net against Hull City in September 1973, scoring from a clearance. He played in 267 games before later reviving his career with rivals Bristol Rovers. John Shaw began his career with Leeds United before following Jimmy Mann to Ashton Gate in May 1974. He helped the club win the Anglo-Scottish Cup in 1977-78 and went on to play in 367 games before joining Exeter City. Keith Waugh who was voted the club's Player of the Year as they reached the League Cup semi-finals in 1988-89, also appeared in two Freight Rover Trophy finals and the promotion play-offs in 1987-88. He made 201 League and Cup appearances before leaving to play for Coventry City. Bolton-born 'keeper Keith Welch joined City from Rochdale in a record £200,000 deal in the summer of 1991. A virtual ever-present in the City side, he helped the club to the Second Division promotion play-offs in 1996-97, going on to make 318 first team appearances.

GOALS

The greatest number of goals Bristol City have ever scored was in their 11-0 victory over Chichester City in the first round of the FA Cup on 5 November 1960. In the League, the club have scored nine goals on two occasions, beating Gillingham 9-4 in 1926-27 and Aldershot 9-0 in 1946-47.

In the club's pre-League days they beat Eastleigh 14-1 in a Western League match.

GOALS - CAREER BEST

The highest goalscorer in the club's history is John Ateyo who between 1951 and 1966 netted 351 goals for the club. These comprised 315 in the League, 30 in the FA Cup, five in the League Cup and one in the Welsh Cup.

GOALS - INDIVIDUAL

'Tot' Walsh holds the club record for the most league goals in a match when he scored six of City's goals in a 9-4 win over Gillingham in a Third Division (South) game on 15 January 1927. Joe Riley scored all five of City's goals in a 5-0 home win over Brighton on 7 February 1934. John Ateyo also scored five goals for the Robins in the 11-0 FA Cup win over Chichester City on 5 November 1960.

GOALS - SEASON
The club's highest league goalscorer in any one season remains Don Clark who scored 36 league goals in 1946-47 as the Robins finished third in Division Three (South). In all games that season, he scored 42 times in only 41 outings.

GOATER, SHAUN
Bermudan international Shaun Goater was spotted by Manchester United during a mid-season break in the Caribbean, signing professional forms for the Old Trafford club in May 1988. Unable to break into the United first team, he moved to Rotherham United but after featuring in the Millers 1991-92 promotion success, he lost form and was loaned to Notts County. In 1994-95 he came into his own, scoring 22 goals for the Millmoor club, whilst the following season he helped them win the Autowindscreen Shield Final at Wembley. Goater had scored 86 goals in 261 games for Rotherham when Bristol City manager Joe Jordan paid £175,000 for him in July 1996.

Goater scored on his City debut in a 3-2 defeat at Gillingham on the opening day of the 1996-97 season and went on to top the scoring charts with 23 goals. This total included a hat-trick in the 4-0 win over Notts County. Goater continued to find the net the following season, scoring another hat-trick in the 3-0 defeat of Wigan Athletic but with City well on the way to clinching promotion, he was sold to Manchester City for £400,000 on transfer deadline day. He had scored 42 goals in 87 League and Cup games but left Ashton Gate saying that he wanted to play a higher grade of football with a bigger team. City finished runners-up to Bristol Rovers and were promoted to the First Division, whilst the Maine Road club were relegated to Division Two!

In 1999-2000, Goater top-scored for City with 29 League and Cup goals, helping Joe Royle's team win promotion to the Premier League.

GOW, GERRY
Gerry Gow was a hard, tough-tackling Scot who joined Bristol City straight from school following his 17th birthday in 1969. He made his debut for the Robins in a 2-1 defeat at Charlton Athletic on the final day of the 1969-70 season before establishing himself as a first team regular the following campaign. Despite his hard man image, justified though it was, Gow was a skilful player. He scored his share of goals too, his best season being 1972-73 when he found the net 15 times in 46 games to top the club's scoring charts. His progress was

monitored by the Scottish international selectors, Gow winning his only Under-23 cap in March 1974 against England at St James Park.

Gow was an ever-present in the Second Division promotion-winning side of 1975-76, City being promoted as runners-up to Sunderland. He continued to be a regular during the four relatively undistinguished seasons in the top flight that followed, ending in relegation in 1980. With another relegation looming, Gow, who had scored 59 goals in 456 League and Cup games was suddenly on his way back to the top flight in October 1980, £175,000 taking him to Maine Road as one of Manchester City manager John Bond's first signings.

Gow's arrival coincided with a dramatic improvement in the Maine Road club's fortunes and he played in all the games in the FA Cup run which ended in the epic final and replay defeat against Tottenham Hotspur.

He lost his place early the following season, moving to Rotherham United in January 1982 for £80,000. In the summer of 1983, John Bond recruited him again, this time for Burnley but he was released after just one season at Turf Moor. Burnley was his final league club but he was later with Yeovil Town for a while as player-manager. Resigning in 1987 he had a spell as Weymouth's manager before ending his involvement with the game.

GUEST PLAYERS

The guest system was used by all clubs during both world wars. Although on occasions it was abused almost beyond belief (some sides that opposed the Robins had ten or 11 guests!) it normally worked sensibly and effectively to the benefit of players, clubs and supporters. City had a number of famous 'guests' playing for them during the Second World War including Jackie Milsom (Manchester City) Ronnie Dix (Tottenham Hotspur) Jack Hargreaves (Leeds United) and Jack Preece (Wolverhampton Wanderers).

GUY, IVOR

Full-back Ivor Guy played his early football for Hambrook Villa before joining Bristol City in 1944. He appeared in 67 wartime games for the Robins before making his league debut in the 4-3 defeat at Aldershot on the opening day of the 1946-47 season.

During the war years, Guy was credited with scoring an incredible goal in the match against Cardiff City, netting from fully 70 yards in the 4-2 win over the Bluebirds. Guy missed very few games over the next 11 seasons, helping the club win the Third Division (South) Championship in 1954-55. It was around this time that Guy became the subject of a bid from First Division Newcastle United but the consistent defender preferred to remain at Ashton Gate.

Guy, who scored three goals in 434 League and Cup games left the Robins in 1958 to play non-League football for Bath City. Sadly his career at Twerton Park was cut short by injury and he was forced into early retirement.

H

HAMILTON, JACK

Jack Hamilton began his career with Ayr United whom he captained to victory in the Ayr Charity Cup on three occasions. He later had spells with Wolves, Derby County and Loughborough before joining Bristol City as they turned professional and entered the Southern League in 1897.

He made his debut at wing-half in the 7-4 win over Wolverton on the opening day of the 1897-98 season. During that campaign he helped the club finish runners-up in the Southern League and win the Western League. The Robins were runners-up in the Southern League again in 1898-99 but after the club had slipped to ninth in 1899-1900, Hamilton, who had scored five goals in 142 games left to join Brentford.

After featuring in the Bees' promotion-winning season of 1900-01 he joined Leeds City before returning to play for Brentford in the summer of 1907. He later moved back to Ashton Gate in charge of City's reserve side. When league football was suspended in 1915, Hamilton took over as manager from George Hedley. Not only did he guide the club through the difficult seasons of wartime football until the appointment of Joe Palmer in 1919 but even turned out twice as an emergency goalkeeper during a player shortage.

HANLIN, PAT

A former Scottish junior international, half-back Pat Hanlin played his early football for Burnbank Athletic before joining Everton. Unable to make the grade with the Goodison Park club, he moved to Bristol City in the summer of 1905.

He made his debut in a 2-1 win at Bradford City in September 1905 though it was towards the end of that 1905-06 season before he won a regular place, helping the club win the Second Division Championship. During his six seasons at Ashton Gate, Hanlin scored just three goals, all in 1906-07 when the club were runners-up in the First Division. Appearing alongside Reuben Marr and Billy Wedlock, Hanlin's performances were such that he was unlucky not to win full international honours. He had scored three goals in 168 games when at the end of the 1910-11 season he decided to retire.

HARDY, BOB
A noted schoolboy footballer, Bob Hardy first played for South Bank Celtic where he won local league honours. On joining South Bank Amateurs, his impressive displays led to him winning an international cap against Wales.

Bristol City manager Harry Thickett signed the pacy winger for the Ashton Gate club in the summer of 1908. After making his debut in a 2-1 home win over Woolwich Arsenal, Hardy missed very few games during his three seasons with the club.

During City's run to the FA Cup Final in 1909, Hardy scored one of the goals in the 2-1 semi-final defeat of Derby County, whilst in the final itself, he was said to be City's best player. Hardy, who scored 15 goals in 85 games, left Ashton Gate after the club were relegated in 1910-11.

HARRIS, JOE
The brother of Newcastle United centre-forward Neil Harris, he began his career with Vale of Clyde, later playing for Glasgow Ashfield before being signed by Burnley. He helped the Clarets finish third in Division Two in 1911-12, the Turf Moor club just missing out on promotion. At the end of that season, Harris joined Bristol City and made his debut for the Robins in a goalless draw against Bradford on the opening day of the 1912-13 season.

Harris, who spent six seasons at Ashton Gate either side of the First World War, was a great provider of chances from which players like Owers, Brown and Howarth scored their fair share of goals. Harris was suspended for twelve months and Bristol City fined £50 after he was paid whilst on amateur forms. He returned to be ever-present in 1920-21 and had scored 28 goals in 218 games when he left to play for Leeds United in the summer of 1922.

At Elland Road he scored 14 goals in 126 games, helping the Yorkshire club win the Second Division Championship in 1923-24. He ended his career with Fulham where he made 42 appearances in two seasons with the Cottagers.

HAT-TRICKS

Alex Caie, who was one of the stars of the first Bristol City professional team, scored a hat-trick in the club's first-ever Southern League game as Wolverton were beaten 7-4, although George Fry holds the record for the club's first hat-trick in an 11-0 win over Swindon Wanderers on 8 September 1894. Jim Blessington scored a hat-trick on his home debut in November 1899 as Cowes were beaten 5-0 but this was later expunged from the records when City's Southern League opponents were forced to disband.

When City beat Dartford 9-2 in an FA Cup replay in 1947-48, Don Clark, Len Townsend and Cyril Williams all scored hat-tricks. Four players have scored hat-tricks on their Football League debut for City. The first was Alfie Rowles in a 4-1 home win over Exeter City on 15 January 1938, going on to set a League record by scoring in each of his first six games. Len Townsend netted a hat-trick on the opening day of the 1947-48 season as Southend United were beaten 6-0. John Galley scored a hat-trick in a 3-0 win at Huddersfield Town on 16 December 1967. In fact, Galley is the only player in the history of the game to have scored hat-tricks when making his debut with two clubs - having previously achieved the feat for Rotherham United at Coventry City in December 1964. The last Bristol City player to achieve the feat was Joe Royle who scored all four goals in the 4-1 win over Middlesbrough on 26 November 1977.

HEDLEY, GEORGE

A robust and aggressive player, George Hedley began his career as an amateur in the Northern League before joining Sheffield United in May 1898. At the end of his first season with the Yorkshire club, Hedley won an FA Cup winners' medal when the Blades beat Derby County 4-1. Three years later he won his second FA Cup winners' medal when United beat Southampton, Hedley scoring the opening goal in a 2-1 win after the first game had been drawn. Hedley, who was capped against Ireland in March 1901, found his career threatened by torn heart muscles but despite medical advice, he refused to give up the game and signed for Southampton

After helping the Saints win the Southern League Championship, he joined Wolves and in his first season netted 11 goals in 37 games including a hat-trick against Burslem Port Vale. The following season of 1907-08 saw Hedley top the club's scoring lists with 16 goals in 22 games including one in the FA Cup

Final against Newcastle United to give him his third FA Cup winners' medal. After seven seasons at Molineux in which he scored 74 goals in 214 games, he left to become manager of Bristol City.

Hedley was in charge at Ashton Gate for the two seasons immediately before the outbreak of the First World War. The club finished eighth in 1913-14 and 18th in 1914-15. He stayed at Ashton Gate until January 1917 when he was called up. After being demobbed he was a Bristol licensee for a good number of years before returning to Wolverhampton where he ran a boarding house.

HEWISON, BOB

Bob Hewison began his playing career with Newcastle United, making 70 first team appearances for the Magpies. On the outbreak of the First World War he began to play for Leeds City and in 1919-20, while recovering from a broken leg, he was asked to act as secretary during the period that the Yorkshire club was being wound up. He returned to St James Park for a brief period before being appointed player-manager of Northampton Town. After five seasons of mid-table mediocrity with the Cobblers, he left to take over the reins at Queen's Park Rangers. Their best season with Hewison in charge was 1929-30 when they finished third in Division Three (South).

He was appointed manager of Bristol City when the club were relegated from the Second Division in 1932. His first spell in charge lasted six seasons, the club's best position during this period being runners-up to Millwall in the Third Division (South) in 1937-38. However, soon afterwards he was suspended for eight months for illegal payments to players. After being employed as the club's chief scout during his suspension, he became manager again in May 1939.

In 1946 he received a long service medal from the Football League but three years later he tendered his resignation following a disagreement with the board over team selection.

He later managed Guildford City and Bath City, taking the Somerset club to the Southern League title in 1959-60.

HIGGINS, SANDY

Joining the club from Grimsby Town, centre-half Sandy Higgins was Bristol City's first captain. He had started his career with Woodfield and then played for Albion Swifts and Birmingham St George's before joining the Mariners.

During his time with Grimsby, for whom he made 126 appearances, Higgins' performances led to him representing the Football League against the Irish League in 1897. One of the Mariners' most versatile players, appearing in almost all outfield positions for the club, he was once presented with a gold medal for ending a season as Town's top scorer with 27 goals.

His first game in Bristol City colours was in the club's first-ever Southern League game, a 7-4 win over Wolverton in which he scored one of the goals. Though he only stayed one season, he made a lasting impression, with his powerful long range shooting being the main feature of his game. He scored 12 goals in 39 games in that season of 1897-98 before leaving to join Newcastle United.

He captained the Magpies after making his debut in their first-ever Division One game. He later played for Middlesbrough before ending his career with Newton Heath just before they changed their name to Manchester United.

HILTON, FRANK

Outside-left Frank Hilton joined City from Doncaster St James in the summer of 1905 and played his first game for the club in a 3-0 win at Lincoln City on 28 October 1905. That season he scored five goals in 26 games as the club won the Second Division Championship, his pin-point crosses providing numerous goalscoring opportunities for Walter Bennett, Willie Maxwell and Sammy Gilligan. The following season he was a regular member of the City side that finished the campaign as runners-up in the First Division. In October 1907, Hilton's performances were rewarded by selection for the Football League against the Irish League at Roker Park where he scored a goal in a 6-3 win. In 1909 he played on the wing in the club's only FA Cup Final appearance when they lost 1-0 to Manchester United. But after just one league appearance the following season, he left the club having scored 22 goals in 128 games.

HINSHELWOOD, WALLY

Wally Hinshelwood began his career with Fulham before he was involved in a part-exchange deal with Jimmy Bowie when moving to Chelsea. He stayed just three months at Stamford Bridge before returning to Fulham. He took his total of appearances for the Cottagers to 19 before he was on the move again, this time to Reading. He spent three seasons at Elm Park and had scored 30 goals in 135 League games when Bristol City manager Pat Beasley paid £15,000 for his services.

He made his debut for the Robins in a 2-1 defeat at Sheffield Wednesday after which he missed very few games for the Ashton Gate club over the next four seasons. Though not a prolific scorer, he created many opportunities for the likes of John Ateyo and Jimmy Rogers. Hinshelwood had scored 19 goals in 158 League and Cup games when following the club's relegation from the Second Division, he left to play for Millwall.

After 19 League appearances for the Lions, he left to try his luck in Canadian football with Toronto Italia before returning to League action with Newport County in November 1961.

His sons Martin and Paul both played for Crystal Palace whilst his grandson Danny Hinshelwood is currently playing for Brighton and Hove Albion after being released by Portsmouth.

HODGSON, ROY

Roy Hodgson was assistant-manager to Bob Houghton at Malmo and Bristol City, moving to Ashton Gate with him in 1980. Hodgson stayed on after Houghton's departure and was in charge from 4 January to 30 April 1982. However, the Robins only won three games out of 20 in this period. The club were also in a dire financial crisis and had to release eight leading professionals from their contracts. When a new company was created at the club, Hodgson's services were dispensed with.

He returned to Sweden to manage Malmo, having many successful years in the 1980s when they regularly appeared in European competitions. Hodgson also took charge of the national team of Switzerland before taking over the reins at Inter Milan.

In June 1997, he was appointed manager of Blackburn Rovers. With Hodgson very active in the transfer market, Rovers finished sixth in the Premier League to secure the club's third appearance in European football in 1998-99. However, after just two wins in the opening 15 League games, it was clear that Hodgson was living on borrowed time and in November 1998, he was relieved of his duties.

HOLLIS, SAM

In his early years, Sam Hollis worked in a Probate Office and the Post Office but in 1894, he was appointed manager of Woolwich Arsenal. After three mediocre seasons, Hollis left to become Bristol City's first manager at the tender age of 31.

The Robins had just been voted into the Southern League and Hollis set about putting together a team. He signed eight new players for just £40 and in his first season in charge, City almost won the Southern League Championship. Hollis resigned in March 1899 after increasing interference from the club's directors. He moved to local rivals Bedminster but when they later amalgamated with Bristol City, Hollis lost his job and left to run his public house.

After Bob Campbell's departure, Hollis was appointed City manager for a second time. After assembling a team for the rigours of the Football League, Hollis' side never finished less than sixth in the Second Division during his four seasons in charge. In 1905, he decided to leave the Ashton Gate club in favour of taking over the Southville Hotel.

Almost six years later, Hollis was back at the helm but the club were in debt and struggled. He left the club after two years to manage Newport County who were playing in the Second Division of the Southern League.

He later became chairman of the Bristol City Shareholders' Association.

HOME MATCHES

The Robins best home victory is the 11-0 first round FA Cup win over Chichester City on 5 November 1960, a match in which John Ateyo scored five of the goals. The club's biggest home win in the Football League occurred on 28 December 1946 when Aldershot were beaten 9-0 with Don Clark scoring four times. In the club's pre-League days, they beat Eastleigh 14-1 in winning the Western League Championship.

The club's worst home defeat is 8-0, a scoreline inflicted upon the Robins by Derby County on 29 September 1923 - not surprisingly the club were relegated to the Third Division at the end of the season.

HOME SEASONS

Bristol City have gone through two Southern League seasons - 1897-98 and 1900-01 - with an undefeated home record. They have failed to achieve that feat in the Football League but have lost just one home match on five occasions - 1903-04, 1905-06, 1922-23 1926-27 and 1937-38.

The club's highest number of home wins in a League seasons is 19. This was achieved in 1926-27 from 21 matches as they won the Championship of the Third Division (South).

HONOURS
The major honours achieved by the club are:

Football League
Division 1 Runners-Up.............1906-07
Division 2 Champions..............1905-06
Division 2 Runners-Up.............1975-76, 1997-98
Division 3(S) Champions 1922-23, 1926-27, 1954-55
Division 3(S) Runners-Up 1937-38
Division 3 Runners-Up 1964-65, 1989-90

FA Cup
Runners-Up 1909
League Cup
Semi-Finalists............................1971, 1989

Welsh Cup
Winners......................................1934

Anglo-Scottish Cup
Winners......................................1978

Freight Rover Trophy
Winners......................................1986
Runners-Up 1987

Autowindscreen Shield
Runners-Up 2000

HOUGHTON, BOB
Bob Houghton started his professional career with Stevenage Town in 1967, later moving to Fulham. Unable to make the grade at Craven Cottage, he joined

Brighton and Hove Albion but again failed to make a League appearance. He qualified as a coach at the age of 20 - one of the youngest in the country - and joined Maidstone United as player-manager. He later spent two years as youth team coach at Ipswich Town before moving to Sweden to manage Malmo.

The Swedish side were runners-up in the European Cup in 1979 after a dreadfully dull game against Nottingham Forest and won the Swedish League title on four occasions. After a short spell in charge of Greek side, Ethnikos, he was appointed manager of Bristol City in October 1980.

Houghton had always longed to manage an English club but with City facing bankruptcy, he resigned in January 1982, after the club had been relegated from Division Two in his first season in charge.

Houghton then managed Toronto Blizzard and they reached two NASL Soccer Bowl finals. He later took charge of Swedish club Orgyte IS.

HUGHES, DICK

Ex-England Schoolboy captain, Dick Hughes was playing as an amateur with Sunderland when Bristol City manager Joe Palmer signed him in September 1920. After a number of impressive performances for the club's reserve side, he finally made his League debut for the Robins at right-back in a 2-0 home win over Coventry City in April 1921. With the exception of a period towards the end of his Ashton Gate career, Dick Hughes was the club's first-choice full-back for ten seasons. He helped City win the Third Division (South) title in 1922-23 and 1926-27 and went on to appear in 280 League and Cup games for the club before leaving at the end of the 1931-32 season to play for Exeter City.

In his first season at St James' Park, Hughes helped the Grecians to finish as runners-up in the Third Division (South). On hanging up his boots, he became the landlord of the 'Old Inn' at Hutton near Weston-super-Mare.

HUNDRED GOALS

Bristol City have scored more than 100 League goals in a season on three occasions. They first achieved the feat in 1926-27 when they scored 104 goals in winning the Third Division (South) Championship. When the club next won the Third Division (South) title in 1954-55 they again passed the hundred goal mark, scoring 101 times. The third and last time the club achieved the feat was 1962-63 when they scored exactly 100 goals in finishing 14th in the Third Division.

HUNTER, NORMAN

Norman 'Bite Yer Legs' Hunter was one of the game's fiercest competitors. Beginning his career with Leeds United, the Elland Road defender renowned for his tackling, relished the reputation that often disguised the fact that he was a very good footballer. He was the first England player to be capped as a substitute when he played against Spain just a few weeks after his full debut against West Germany. Only the presence of England captain Bobby Moore stopped him from earning more international honours than his 28 caps. Hunter was

Norman Hunter

remarkably consistent, playing in five ever-present seasons and featuring in all Leeds' Cup Finals from 1965 to 1975. During that time he won two League Championship medals, an FA Cup winners' medal, League Cup winners' medal and two Inter Cities Fairs Cup winners' medals. Hunter also had the honour of being voted the PFA's first-ever Player of the Year in 1973.

In October 1976, he joined Bristol City and made his debut in a 2-0 defeat at Derby County, going on to appear in 41 consecutive League games before injury ruined the sequence. A firm favourite with the Ashton Gate crowd, Hunter went on to score four goals in 108 League games in three seasons with the club before being appointed player-coach with Barnsley under Allan Clarke. When Clarke left to manage Leeds, Hunter took over at Oakwell but after steering them into Division Two, he was surprisingly sacked. He later had a spell as assistant-manager at West Bromwich Albion before going to Rotherham United as manager. After being dismissed in December 1987, he joined the Leeds United coaching staff but lost his job when Howard Wilkinson was sacked. He had a brief spell as Terry Yorath's assistant at Bradford City but now works works as a summariser for BBC Radio Leeds.

HUTCHINSON, BOBBY

Much-travelled Scottish midfielder Bobby Hutchinson began his career as a striker with Montrose before joining Dundee in the summer of 1974. After three seasons at Dens Park, he moved to Hibernian in exchange for Eric Schaedler and in 1979 he played in the Scottish Cup Final for the Easter Road club.

In July 1980 he came south of the border to play for Football League newcomers, Wigan Athletic. After just one season at Springfield Park, Hutchinson joined Tranmere Rovers but it wasn't long before he was on his way to Mansfield Town. In January 1984 he rejoined the Prenton Park club, taking his total of League appearances in his two spells with the club to 56. Bristol City manager Terry Cooper signed him on a free transfer and he made his debut as a substitute for Rob Newman in a 1-1 draw at Doncaster Rovers. Appointed club captain, he led the side to success in the Freight Rover Trophy as City beat Bolton Wanderers 3-0 in the Wembley final in 1986. He went on to score 11 goals in 105 League and Cup games before joining Walsall in February 1987.

He later had loan spells with Blackpool and Carlisle United before returning to live in Scotland.

I

INQUIRY
Celebrations following the club's successful Third Division (South) Championship-winning season of 1922-23 were cut short by an FA Inquiry into the dealings of the club. Six of City's directors were suspended for life from any involvement in running a football club, manager Alex Raisbeck was fined £50 and the club £250. The bans remained in force for three years but in January 1926 following arduous campaigning by Raisbeck, the bans were lifted.

INTERNATIONAL MATCHES
Ashton Gate has been host to two full international matches involving England. The first was on Monday 20 March 1899 when the ground was then the home of Bedminster. A crowd of 6,000 watched England beat Wales 4-0 with goals from Steve Bloomer(2) Fred Forman and Ernie Needham.

The two sides met again at Ashton Gate on Monday 17 March 1913 when the ground was the home of Bristol City. This time a crowd of 9,000 saw a much closer game with England winning 4-3. Former Bristol City 'keeper Bailiff was in the Welsh goals whilst Billy Wedlock, City's centre-half was selected for the England team but was forced to withdraw because of injury.

INTERNATIONAL PLAYERS
Bristol City's most capped player (ie: caps gained while players were registered with the club) is Billy Wedlock with 26 caps. The following is a complete list of players who have gained full international honours while at Ashton Gate.

England	*Wales*
John Ateyo 6	Mark Aizlewood 21
Joe Cottle 1	Rob Edwards 4
Billy Jones 1	John Emanuel 5

Billy Wedlock 26   Billy Matthews 1
                                  Howard Pritchard 1
                                  Bertie Williams 1
Republic of Ireland
Dermot Curtis 5

City's first player to be capped was Billy Jones when he played for England v Ireland at The Dell in March 1901.

J

JACOBS, TREVOR

Trevor Jacobs had a disastrous debut for the Robins, scoring an own goal in a 3-3 draw at Rotherham United in November 1966. His only other appearance in the City side that season was in the return match with the Millers towards the end of the campaign. It was midway through the 1967-68 season that Jacobs displaced Tony Ford in the City side on a regular basis. His first goal for the club was the only one in the game against Carlisle United in September 1967. Jacobs missed very few games over the next five seasons, helping the Robins reach the League Cup semi-finals in 1970-71.

After losing his place, he had a brief loan spell with Plymouth Argyle before joining Bristol Rovers on a free transfer in May 1973. The following season he was ever-present as the then Eastville club won promotion to the Second Division. On leaving League football, Jacobs played for Bideford, Paulton Rovers and Clevedon Town before hanging up his boots.

JONES, BILLY

The first player to win international recognition whilst on Bristol City's books, Billy Jones was capped by England against Ireland at The Dell in March 1901. Originally a forward with Heaton Rovers, Willington Athletic and Loughborough Town, he became the first player to be signed by Bristol City manager Sam Hollis.

His first game for the Robins was in a 2-2 draw at Gravesend United and though he struggled to score in the Southern League, he scored four times in the club's 14-1 Western League win over Eastleigh.

After a season playing at wing-half, he was switched back to the forward line for the 1899-1900 season and responded with 24 goals including four in the 5-1 home defeat of Sheppey United. Jones' career with City spanned the club's election to the Football League but after scoring 51 goals in 339 games, he joined Spurs as cover for the club's regular half-back line of Ted Hughes, Tom

Morris and Walter Bull. After just one season at White Hart Lane he left to join Swindon Town with whom he ended his career.

JORDAN, JOE

Joe Jordan began his footballing days with Morton before Leeds United paid £15,000 to bring him to Elland Road in October 1970 after he had made just ten League appearances. Within a couple of years, he was leading the Yorkshire side's assault on the League Championship. He later played in two European finals and won his first Scottish cap before Manchester United paid £350,000 for him in January 1978.

One of the most feared strikers in the First Division, his strength lay in his ability to unsettle defenders and pressurise goalkeepers. In all, he played 125 games for United, scoring 41 goals Jordan was a regular choice as Scotland's centre-forward and is the only Scot to have scored in three World Cup Finals.

In 1980 he moved to AC Milan and then Verona before returning to the Football League with Southampton in the summer of 1984. He ended the season as the club's leading scorer but his courageous style of play could not take the Saints any higher than fifth place in Division One. After suffering a series of injuries, Jordan left the Dell to join Bristol City as the Ashton Gate club's player-coach, eventually becoming their manager.

He plotted the club's 1988-89 League Cup run and their promotion success the following season but in September 1990 after scoring 12 goals in 72 games, he left Ashton Gate to manage Hearts. After a spell as Liam Brady's assistant at Celtic, Jordan managed Stoke City before returning to Ashton Gate for a second spell in charge in November 1994. The popular Scot left the Robins by mutual consent in March 1997, having a spell as assistant to then Northern Ireland manager Lawrie McMenemy.

JUBILEE FUND

The League Benevolent Fund was launched in 1938, fifty years after the start of the Football League, to benefit players who had fallen on hard times. It was decided that the best way to raise funds was for sides to play local derby games with no account being taken of League status.

On 20 August 1938, City entertained Bristol Rovers but went down 3-1 with Willshaw scoring their goal. On 19 August 1939, Rovers also won the second Jubilee Fund game at Eastville 4-0.

Joe Jordan

K

KEATING, ALBERT

Albert Keating joined Newcastle United from Prudhoe Castle but in two years at St James' Park, he only made 12 appearances. In November 1925 he joined Bristol City and scored twice on his debut in a 5-1 home win over Luton Town. In fact, Keating scored in each of his first four games for the club, ending his first season at Ashton Gate with eight goals in 19 games.

Forming a prolific goalscoring partnership with 'Tot' Walsh in 1926-27, he helped the club win the Third Division (South) Championship, his total of 23 goals including hat-tricks in the wins over Crystal Palace (Home 5-4) and Luton Town (Home 6-0). In 1927-28 he was the club's leading scorer with 16 goals in 25 games including another hat-trick in a 5-1 home win over Clapton Orient. It was this kind of form that prompted FA Cup winners Blackburn Rovers to pay £4,000 for his services in May 1928.

However, the Ewood Park club were in the First Division and Keating struggled to win a regular place, making just 17 appearances in three seasons with the Lancashire club.

At the end of the 1930-31 season, Keating joined Cardiff City and though he had a disappointing first term at Ninian Park, he scored 23 goals in 38 games in 1931-32 including a hat-trick in an 8-0 FA Cup win over Enfield.

He returned to play for a brief spell with Bristol City, taking his tally of goals to 54 in 104 League and Cup games before leaving to play non-League football with North Shields.

KELSO, BOB

Scottish international Bob Kelso first made his name with Renton when they were one of the top teams north of the border. In the close season of 1888, he moved to Newcastle West End but within a few months he had joined Everton. He made his debut against Preston North End towards the end of the club's first season in the Football League. He then left Everton to play for Preston North End and in two seasons with the Deepdale club, made 38 League appearances. Kelso was a fine defender, completely at home at full-back as well as wing-half. In the summer of 1891 he rejoined Everton and was a member of the side which lost to Wolverhampton Wanderers in the 1893 FA Cup Final. In 1894-95 he was instrumental in Everton ending the season as runners-up to Sunderland in the First Division. He played in 103 first team games for Everton before joining Dundee in the 1896 close season, winning further international caps.

In 1898 Kelso moved to Bedminster where he became the club's first captain. He made his debut in a 4-1 win at Trowbridge Town in the Western League and though he only stayed with the club for one season, his experience shone through. Kelso's only goal for the club came in the Southern League in a 2-2 draw at Sheppey United. He appeared in 38 games for Bedminster before hanging up his boots.

L

LARGEST CROWD
It was on 16 February 1935 that Ashton Gate housed its largest crowd. The occasion was the FA Cup fifth round match against Preston North End. A staggering crowd of 43,335 saw the teams play out a goalless draw.

LATE FINISHES
Bristol City's final match of the season against Crystal Palace at Selhurst Park on 24 May 1947 is the latest date for the finish of any Robins' season apart from during the war. For the record, the game was goalless. During the war many curious things occurred, among them the continuance of the 1939-40 season into June. Thus, City's last competitive match in that campaign was on 8 June when they lost 4-1 at Swansea Town.

LEADING GOALSCORERS
Bristol City have provided the Football League's divisional leading goalscorer on three occasions:

1946-47	Don Clark	Division Three(South)	36 goals
1947-48	Len Townsend	Division Three(South)	31 goals
1989-90	Bob Taylor	Division Three	27 goals

LEAGUE GOALS - CAREER HIGHEST
John Ateyo holds the Ashton Gate record for the most League goals with a career total of 315 goals between 1951 and 1966.

LEAGUE GOALS - LEAST CONCEDED
During the 1905-06 season, the Robins conceded just 28 goals when winning the Second Division Championship.

LEAGUE GOALS - MOST INDIVIDUAL
Don Clark holds the Bristol City record for the most League goals in a season. He scored 36 in the 1946-47 season when the Robins finished third in Division Three (South).

LEAGUE GOALS - MOST SCORED
Bristol City's highest goals tally in the Football League was during the Third Division (South) Championship-winning season of 1926-27 when they scored 104 goals.

LEAGUE VICTORY - HIGHEST
Bristol City's best League victory is the 9-0 win over Aldershot at Ashton Gate on 28 December 1946. Don Clark scored four of the goals and Jack Hargreaves netted a hat-trick whilst City's other scorers were Ernie Jones and Cyril Williams.

LENNARTSSON, BENNY
Benny Lennartsson, technical director to Sweden's 1994 World Cup squad replaced John Ward as Bristol City's manager in 1998. Unfortunately, despite all his experience, he was unable to prevent the Robins from returning to the Second Division after just one season in Division One. City ended the 1998-99 season bottom of the Second Division, five points adrift of safety and Lennartsson lost his job, being replaced by Tony Pulis.

LEYLAND DAF CUP
A competition designed solely and specifically for the Associate Members of the Football League, the Leyland Daf Cup replaced the Sherpa Van Trophy for the 1989-90 season. The Robins were unbeaten in their group games, beating Swansea City (Home 2-1) and drawing with Reading (Away 1-1). However, the Ashton Gate club went out of the competition in the first round, losing 1-0 at home to Notts County.

LLEWELLYN, ANDY
A former England Youth international, Bristol-born defender Andy Llewellyn made his City debut in a 1-0 defeat at Rochdale in December 1982, only a few months after joining the club as an apprentice. Although he only made 10 first team appearances over the next two seasons, Andy Llewellyn became an impor-

tant member of the City side. He appeared in the 1987 Freight Rover Trophy Final against Mansfield Town and the following season's promotion play-offs. In 1989-90, Llewellyn was one of only two ever-presents as the Robins won promotion to the Second Division as runners-up to Bristol Rovers. In Division Two, Llewellyn was the club's most outstanding player and it came as no surprise when he was voted Player of the Year.

Llewellyn, who scored the first of his three goals for the club in a 4-0 win at Bolton Wanderers in April 1986, made 351 League and Cup appearances before following a loan spell with Exeter City, he left to join Yeovil Town.

LONG SERVICE
Right-half Cliff Morgan still holds the record as Bristol City's longest-serving player. After joining the Ashton Gate club as an amateur in September 1930, he made his League debut at Tottenham Hotspur on 12 March 1932 and played the last of his 280 first team games against Swindon Town on 19 February 1949. Towards the end of his career he became player-coach but on hanging up his boots, he was appointed the club's chief scout, serving the Robins for over 45 years.

LOW, GORDON
Aberdeen-born wing-half Gordon Low followed his school friend Denis Law to Huddersfield town but was unable to make the grade with the then Leeds Road club and in March 1961 he joined Bristol City for £3,000.

Low made his Robins' debut in a 4-1 home win over Watford and though early the following season he scored his first goal for the club - the winner in a 4-3 defeat of Peterborough United - it was 1963-64 before he won a regular place in the City side.

In 1964-65 he was appointed club captain and led the Robins to promotion to the Second Division as runners-up to Carlisle United. Low, who was ever-present that season and in 1965-66 appeared in 136 consecutive League games but when Fred Ford left the club, he found he was no longer guaranteed first team football.

Having scored 17 goals in 226 League and Cup games, he left Ashton Gate to play for Stockport County in the summer of 1978. He made 73 appearances for the Hatters before joining Crewe Alexandra where he ended his League career.

He later played non-League football for Selby Town and worked part-time as Huddersfield Town's youth coach.

LOWEST

The lowest number of goals scored by Bristol City in a single Football League season is 29 in 1980-81 when the club finished 21st in the Second Division and were relegated. The club's lowest points record in the Football League occurred in 1931-32 when the Robins gained just 23 points and were relegated from the Second Division.

LUMSDEN, JIMMY

Jimmy Lumsden began his career with Leeds United but opportunities at Elland Road were rare and in September 1970 he joined Southend United. He signed for Morton in 1971 and was ever-present the following season. In December 1972 he joined St Mirren, then played for Cork Hibernians before rejoining Morton in 1973. In the summer of 1975 he signed for Clydebank and won a Scottish League Division Two medal in his first season and promotion to the Premier Division the following year. He was Celtic's youth team manager before rejoining Leeds United as assistant-manager to Eddie Gray. The pair were dismissed in October 1985 but linked up again at Rochdale in December 1986.

In September 1990, Lumsden joined Bristol City as assistant-manager to Joe Jordan and took over when Jordan moved to Scotland to manage Hearts. The 1990-91 season was one of consolidation for the Robins but midway through the following campaign with City lying 20th in the Second Division, after just one win in 14 games, Lumsden was sacked.

M

MABBUTT, KEVIN

Hailing from a footballing family, his father Ray playing for Bristol Rovers and Newport County and brother Gary for Bristol Rovers, Spurs and England, Kevin was an England Youth international. He made his League debut for the Robins in a 1-0 defeat at Nottingham Forest in the second game of the 1977-78 season, going on to score four goals in 26 appearances. The following season he netted a hat-trick in a 3-1 win at Manchester United as City went on to finish 13th in the First Division. In 1980-81 Mabbutt was the club's leading scorer and was voted Player of the Year. He scored in all rounds of the FA Cup including City's goal in the 2-1 fifth round defeat at Nottingham Forest.

He had scored 39 goals in 149 League and Cup games when in October 1981 he left to join Crystal Palace in a £200,000 exchange deal involving Terry Boyle.

Leading marksman in successive seasons at Selhurst Park, he had scored 22 goals in 75 League games before injury curtailed his career. He later had brief spells playing in Canada, Belgium and Cyprus but is now living in California where he runs his family restaurant called 'Delicias'.

MANAGERS

Below is the full list of Bristol City's full-time managers with the dates in which they held office:

Sam Hollis	April 1897 - April 1899
Bob Campbell	May 1899 - June 1901
Sam Hollis	June 1901 - April 1905
Harry Thickett	May 1905 - October 1910
Frank Bacon	October 1910 - January 1911
Sam Hollis	January 1911 - April 1913
George Hedley	April 1913 - January 1917

Jack Hamilton	January 1917 - May 1919
Joe Palmer	May 1919 - October 1921
Alex Raisbeck	December 1921 - July 1929
Joe Bradshaw	August 1929 - February 1932
Bob Hewison	April 1932 - September 1938
Clarrie Bourton	October 1938 - May 1939
Bob Hewison	May 1939 - March 1949
Bob Wright	April 1949 - June 1950
Pat Beasley	July 1950 - January 1958
Peter Doherty	January 1958 - March 1960
Fred Ford	July 1960 - September 1967
Alan Dicks	October 1967 - September 1980
Bob Houghton	October 1980 - January 1982
Roy Hodgson	January 1982 - April 1982
Terry Cooper	May 1982 - March 1988
Joe Jordan	March 1988 - September 1990
Jimmy Lumsden	September 1990 - February 1992
Denis Smith	March 1992 - January 1993
Russell Osman	January 1993 - November 1994
Joe Jordan	November 1994 - March 1997
John Ward	March 1997 - October 1998
Benny Lennartsson	October 1998 - July 1999
Tony Pulis	July 1999 - December 1999
Tony Fawthorp	January 2000 - May 2000
Danny Wilson	June 2000 -

MANN, GEORGE

Half-back George Mann first came to prominence with his local club, East Stirling before joining Blackburn Rovers. After gaining First Division experience with the Ewood Park club, Mann moved to Manchester City. In 1895-96, Mann helped the Maine Road side reach the promotion Test Matches but in the summer of 1897 after scoring seven goals in 58 league games, he joined Bristol City.

Mann played his first game for the club in the 7-4 win over Wolverton, helping the Robins finish as runners-up in the Southern League and win the Western League. After just one more season with the club, in which they again finished runners-up in the Southern League, Mann, who had scored 13 goals in 41 games in that competition, was forced to retire following an injury received in the game against Chatham in January 1899.

MANN, JIMMY

Midfielder Jimmy Mann played for Yorkshire Schoolboys before joining Leeds United as an apprentice and turning professional in December 1969. After finding his first team opportunities at Elland Road limited, Mann joined Bristol City on a free transfer.

He made his debut for the Robins in a goalless draw at Nottingham Forest on the opening day of the 1974-75 season. The following campaign he was a key player as City won promotion to the First Division as runners-up to Sunderland. Mann, who scored a number of vital goals during his stay at Ashton Gate, netted two in the 3-0 second leg win over Partick Thistle to give City a 3-2 victory in the quarter-final of the 1977-78 Anglo-Scottish Cup, which they went on to win.

As City hit deep financial trouble, Mann was one of the eight players who agreed to have their contracts cancelled to help save the club. After scoring 46 goals in 283 games he was signed for Barnsley in February 1982 by Norman Hunter. In December of that year he joined Scunthorpe United on a non-contract basis and in February 1983 went to Doncaster Rovers on a free transfer. He later played non-League football for Goole Town where he now lives, working as a marine operator at the town's docks.

MARATHON MATCHES

On 14 April 1945, the Robins met Cardiff City in a War League Cup second round second leg tie at Ninian Park. After 90 minutes, City had won 2-1 to make the scores level as the Welsh team had won by the same scoreline at Ashton Gate. After extra-time, some spectators went home for their tea before returning to see the tie go to sudden death. Eventually after 3 hours 22 minutes, Billy Rees scored the winner for Cardiff City.

Bristol City met Aldershot in the FA Cup second round on 10 December 1988 at the Recreation Ground. Aldershot led 1-0 until Carl Shutt equalised in injury time. The replay at Ashton Gate three days later finished goalless after extra-time. Then it was back to Aldershot on 20 December. The Shots again led 1-0 when Shutt equalised in injury time to force extra-time. The game finished 2-2 and two days later it was back to Ashton Gate for the third replay. A goal by Shutt after just ten minutes settled the tie which took 420 minutes to complete!

103

MARKSMEN - LEAGUE

The Robins' top League goalscorer is John Ateyo who struck 315 goals during his 15 seasons at Ashton Gate. Only four players have hit more than 100 League goals for the club.

1. John Ateyo 315
2. Arnold Rodgers 106
3. Tom Ritchie 102
4. Jimmy Rogers 102
5. Tot Walsh 88
6. John Galley 84
7. Brian Clark 83
8. Sammy Gilligan 78
9. Alan Walsh 77
10. Bobby Williams 76

MARKSMEN - OVERALL

In all games, four players have hit a century of goals for Bristol City. The club's top marksman is John Ateyo. The Century Club consists of:

1. John Ateyo 351
2. Tom Ritchie 132
3. Arnold Rodgers 111
4. Jimmy Rogers 108

MARR, REUBEN

Doncaster-born right-half Reuben Marr developed his skills in his home-town junior soccer leagues before joining Mexborough Town. His performances for the Yorkshire League club led to City manager Harry Thickett signing him in the summer of 1906.

He made his debut for the Robins in a 2-2 draw at Birmingham, going on to appear in 30 games as City finished runners-up to Newcastle United in the First Division. Settling in well alongside Billy Wedlock and Pat Hanlin, he helped the club reach the FA Cup Final in 1908-09. Though he was given a benefit match against Burnley in February 1913 after seven seasons service, he was still a member of the first team when League football resumed after the hostilities in 1919.

In 1919-20 he appeared in the FA Cup second round game against Arsenal (Home 1-0) as City reached the semi-finals before losing to Huddersfield Town. At the end of the season, Marr, who had scored 11 goals in 194 League and Cup outings, finally hung up his boots.

MATCH OF THE DAY
Bristol City's first appearance on BBC's 'Match of the Day' was on 5 February 1966 when they drew 1-1 against Manchester City at Ashton Gate with Brian Clark scoring the home side's goal.

MAXWELL, WILLIE
Willie Maxwell began his career with his home-town club Arbroath before joining Heart of Midlothian. When he was 18, he turned professional and came south of the border to play for Stoke. Eventually he moved back to Scotland and was playing for Third Lanark when Sunderland persuaded him to join them. His stay at Roker Park was brief and he moved to Millwall. It was July 1905 when Harry Thickett signed the much-travelled forward.

He made his debut for City at Manchester United on the opening day of the 1905-06 season, scoring the club's only goal in a 5-1 defeat. Forming an effective striking partnership with Sammy Gilligan and Walter Bennett, Maxwell was the club's top scorer with 25 goals in 38 games as they won the Second Division Championship. His total included hat-tricks in the wins over Burton United (Home 4-0) and Stockport County (Home 7-0). He topped the club's scoring charts again in 1906-07 and had netted 62 goals in 128 games when he left the Robins in the summer of 1909 to coach Leopold of Brussels and later the Belgian national team in the 1912 Olympic Games.

MERRICK, GEOFF
An England Schoolboys captain, Geoff Merrick signed professional forms in August 1968, three months after making his League debut in a 4-2 win at Aston Villa. However, it was towards the end of the 1970-71 season before Merrick won a regular place in the City side, appearing in just seven league games over the previous three seasons. Midway through the 1971-72 season, in which he was ever-present, Merrick was appointed club captain, leading the team for the first time against Blackpool at Bloomfield Road. Always leading by example, he was outstanding in the club's run to the sixth round of the FA Cup in 1973-74.

Merrick was ever-present in seasons 1974-75 and 1975-76, appearing in 99 consecutive league games during that spell and leading the club to promotion to the First Division in the latter of these seasons. During the club's first season in the top flight, Merrick was switched to left-back to accommodate Norman Hunter. Merrick had missed very few games since establishing himself in the City side but in the summer of 1978 he suffered a pelvic strain which kept him out of the first team for the whole of the following season.

He was back in action at the start of the 1979-80 season, his inspirational performances leading to him being voted the club's Player of the Year for a second time. Merrick's career with the club was eventually cut short by the 'Ashton Gate Eight' crisis in 1982. Merrick had scored 13 goals in 414 League and Cup games when he left City to play for Yeovil Town.

He later had a spell playing for Carolina Hills of Hong Kong before turning out for a number of non-League clubs including Bath City, Gloucester City and Minehead.

MONTEITH, HUGH

Goalkeeper Hugh Monteith played his early football in his native Scotland for Parkhead Juniors before signing for Celtic. After just one season there, he joined Loughborough Town, moving to Bristol City in the summer of 1897.

Over the next three seasons, Monteith, who made his debut in a 7-4 home win over Wolverton on the opening day of the 1897-98 Southern League season, showed his consistency. He was ever-present that season as the newly named City finished as runners-up in the Southern League and won the Western League title. He had appeared in 139 games for the Ashton Gate club when in the 1900 close season, he moved to West Ham United. He made 60 Southern League and FA Cup appearances for the Hammers before joining Bury.

His performances for the Shakers were outstanding and in 1903 when the Gigg Lane club won the FA Cup, beating Derby County 6-0, the Ayrshire-born 'keeper went through the competition without conceding a single goal.

MORGAN, CLIFF

One of the club's longest-serving players, Cliff Morgan was playing for Bristol Boys Brigade when spotted by the Ashton Gate club. When he joined City, Morgan was an inside-forward and it was in this position that he made his debut in a 2-1 defeat at Spurs in March 1932. Switched to half-back, Morgan was one of the leading players in the club's run to the fifth round of the FA Cup in 1934-35. During the club's promotion near-miss in 1937-38 Morgan missed just one game, scoring a spectacular goal in the 4-2 home win over Southend United.

Appointed club captain, he was still the Robins' first-choice wing-half when League football resumed in 1946-47, having appeared in 203 wartime games.

In April 1948 he became City's player-coach, playing the last of his 267 League and Cup games against Swindon Town on 19 February 1949 at the age of 35. He later became City's chief scout and went on to give outstanding service to the club for 45 years.

MOST GOALS IN A SEASON

When Bristol City won the Third Division (South) Championship in 1926-27, they scored 104 goals in 42 matches with Tommy 'Tot' Walsh top-scoring with 32 goals.

MOST MATCHES

Bristol City played their greatest number of matches in season 1988-89 when they played 64. This comprised 46 league games, six FA Cup games, nine Football League Cup games and three Sherpa Van Trophy games.

MOYES, DAVID

Former Scottish Youth international defender David Moyes began his career with Celtic where he helped the Parkhead club win the League Championship in 1981-82 and gained European Cup experience the following season.

In October 1983 he joined Cambridge United, making 86 appearances before moving to Bristol City for a fee of £10,000 in October 1985. He made his Robins' debut in a 4-0 defeat at Notts County but after City lost 6-3 at Bury two games later, he lost his place until recovering his form at the turn of the year. He helped the club win the Freight Rover Trophy in 1986 and went on to appear in 94 games before leaving to join Shrewsbury Town in October 1987. Ever-present with the Gay Meadow club in 1989-90 he then had spells with Dunfermline Athletic and Hamilton Academicals before joining Preston North End.

Initially the Deepdale club's captain and coach, he was outstanding in their Third Division title success in 1995-96 and went on to appear in 160 League and Cup games before being appointed the Lancashire club's manager in January 1998, and leading them to promotion to the first Division in 1999-2000.

N

NEESAM, BERT

One of the club's longest-serving players, wing-half Bert Neesam played his early football for his village side Brompton in the Northallerton League of Yorkshire. He was the club's leading marksman and had won three winners' medals before leaving to play for Grangetown Athletic in the Northern League. His impressive performances led to him joining Bristol City in September 1913, making his debut in a 1-1 draw at Glossop six months later. In 1914-15, Neesam scored 10 goals in 19 games including a hat-trick in a 3-2 win at Grimsby Town. He played throughout the war years and was a regular first team member until 1927-28.

During that time he helped the club win the Third Division (South) Championship in 1922-23 and 1926-27. Appointed the Robins' captain, Bert Neesam scored 19 goals in 297 League and Cup games before leaving Ashton Gate in the summer of 1928 to play non-League football for Bath City, where he later ended his career.

NEUTRAL GROUNDS

Ashton Gate has been used as a neutral ground for FA Cup matches on a number of occasions and as early as 1899 staged an international match when England beat Wales 4-0. City's ground played host to another England v Wales international in 1913 when the home side won 4-3. The ground has also housed five England Under-23 matches. Bristol City themselves have had to replay on a neutral ground in the FA Cup a number of times.

Date	*Opponents*	*Venue*	*FA Cup*	*Score*
14.01.1901	Reading	Swindon	Round 1	1-2
31.03.1909	Derby County	St Andrew's	Semi-Final	2-1
21.01.1935	Bury	Villa Park	Round 3	2-1

The club's two appearances in the semi-finals were of course played on neutral grounds.

Date	Opponents	Venue	Score
27.03.1909	Derby County	Stamford Bridge	1-1
27.03.1920	Huddersfield Town	Stamford Bridge	1-2

During the club's successful Welsh Cup campaign of 1933-34, City beat Port Vale 1-0 at Sealand Road in the semi-final and after drawing 1-1 against Tranmere Rovers at the Racecourse Ground in the final, won 3-0 in the replay also at Sealand Road.

The club's appearances in the FA Cup Final at the Crystal Palace and the Freight Rover Trophy Final at Wembley also qualify for inclusion.

NEVILLE, STEVE

A former Southampton apprentice, Steve Neville played five games for the Saints during their 1977-78 promotion campaign before being sold to Exeter City for £20,000 in September 1978. His impressive performances for the Grecians led to Sheffield United paying £80,000 for his services in October 1980. Having helped the Blades win the Fourth Division Championship in 1981-82, Neville rejoined Exeter until City manager Terry Cooper exchanged Trevor Morgan for him in November 1984.

Neville made his Bristol City debut in a 2-1 home win over Lincoln City, ending the season with eight goals in 28 games. In 1985-86 he was the club's leading scorer with 19 goals, forming a prolific striking partnership with Alan Walsh. Also that season he helped City win the Freight Rover Trophy, making two of the goals in the 3-0 win over Bolton Wanderers at Wembley. He went on to score 46 goals in 148 League and Cup games before following Terry Cooper to St James Park for a third spell with Exeter City. An important member of the Grecians side that won the Fourth Division Championship in 1989-90, he has since played in Hong Kong and for a number of non-League sides.

NEWMAN, ROB

Beginning his career with Bristol City, Rob Newman entered the game early due to the crisis which threatened the Ashton Gate club's very existence in 1982. He made his debut for the Robins in the match against Fulham (Home

0-0) immediately after the departure of the 'Ashton Gate Eight'. A versatile central defender he was an influential member of the City side that won promotion in 1983-84, reached two Freight Rover Trophy finals and the League Cup semi-finals of 1988-89. An ever-present on three occasions and the club's Player of the Year in 1986-87, he captained the Robins to promotion in 1989-90 before having scored 59 goals in 483 games, he left to join Norwich City for £600,000 in July 1991.

Good in the air and dangerous at set pieces, he scored a number of vital goals for the Canaries in his seven seasons at Carrow Road, perhaps none more so than his 89th minute goal at Barnsley in April 1996 to secure a vital point in a 2-2 draw as the club narrowly avoided consecutive relegations.

Though he wore eight different numbered shirts in his 249 first team appearances for the Canaries, it was as a defender, especially when playing alongside John Polsten, that he gave his best performances.

After loan spells with Motherwell and Wigan Athletic, Newman joined Southend United on a free transfer in the summer of 1998.

NICHOLSON, JOCK

Jock Nicholson began his career with Glasgow Ashfield before Bristol City manager Sam Hollis signed him in the summer of 1911. The tough-tackling left-half made his City debut in a 1-0 home win over Fulham on the opening day of the 1911-12 season. Nicholson was a virtual ever-present in the City side up until the outbreak of the First World War, scoring his first goal for the club against Birmingham in December 1914.

When League football resumed in 1919, Nicholson had replaced Billy Wedlock as City's captain and impressed in the club's run to the semi-final of the FA Cup in 1919-20. The following season he was an influential member of the side that almost won promotion to the top flight but had to settle for third place in Division Two. He had taken his tally of goals to four in 207 League and Cup games when he left Ashton Gate to join Glasgow Rangers in July 1921.

After a year at Ibrox he moved to St Johnstone but following a spell as coach to Swiss club Etoile-Carouse, he rejoined Bristol City as the club's trainer. He later held a similar post with Manchester United before ending his involvement with the game coaching in Sweden.

NICKNAMES

Bristol City's nickname is the Robins. Many players in the club's history have been fondly known by their nicknames. Some of the more unusual include:

Walter Leigh	1902-1903	Swappy
Walter Bennett	1905-1907	Cocky
Billy Wedlock	1905-1921	India Rubber Man
Albert Fairclough	1921-1924	Fairy
Ernie Peacock	1946-1959	Ginger
Rob Newman	1918-1991	Biff

NON-LEAGUE

Bristol City have played non-League opposition in the FA Cup on a number of occasions. The most recent was the second round tie at home to St Albans City on 6 December 1996 when the Robins won 9-2. City's record against non-League clubs in the FA Cup since the Second World War is outstanding and is as follows:

Date	*Opposition*	*Venue*	*Stage*	*Score*
30.11.1946	Hayes	Home	Round 1	9-3
29.11.1947	Dartford	Away	Round 1	0-0
06.12.1947	Dartford	Home	Round 1R	9-2
25.11.1950	Gloucester City	Home	Round 1	4-0
02.12.1953	Rhyl	Away	Round 2	3-0
26.01.1957	Rhyl	Home	Round 4	3-0
05.11.1960	Chichester City	Home	Round 1	11-0
26.11.1960	King's Lynn	Away	Round 2	2-2
29.11.1960	King's Lynn	Home	Round 2R	3-0
04.11.1961	Hereford United	Home	Round 1	1-1
08.11.1961	Hereford United	Away	Round 1R	5-2
25.11.1961	Dartford	Home	Round 2	8-2
03.11.1962	Wellington Town	Home	Round 1	4-2
24.11.1962	Wimbledon	Home	Round 2	2-1
16.11.1963	Corby Town	Away	Round 1	3-1
19.11.1983	Corinthian Casuals	Away	Round 1	0-0
23.11.1983	Corinthian Casuals	Home	Round 1R	4-0

17.11.1984	Fisher Athletic	Away	Round 1	1-0
15.11.1986	VS Rugby	Home	Round 1	3-1
06.12.1986	Bath City	Home	Round 2	1-1
09.12.1986	Bath City	Home	Round 2R	3-0
14.11.1987	Aylesbury United	Home	Round 1	1-0
18.11.1989	Barnet	Home	Round 1	2-0
06.12.1996	St Albans City	Home	Round 2	9-2

O

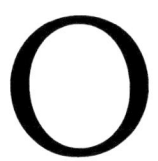

O'BRIEN, PADDY

Paddy O'Brien began his career in Glasgow junior football with Elm Park and Glasgow Northern before signing for Woolwich Arsenal in April 1894. In the first of his three seasons with the club he scored 11 goals in 27 games including a hat-trick against Burslem Port Vale on Christmas Day 1894. A serious injury on the opening day of the 1895-96 season resulted in O'Brien missing four months action. He regained his place in January 1896 and the following season was the club's leading scorer with 14 goals in 26 league games. He had scored 29 goals in 67 games when he was transferred to Bristol City during the summer of 1897.

He made his debut in a 7-4 home win over Wolverton on the opening day of the 1897-98 Southern League season, helping the club to end the campaign as runners-up, a feat they repeated the following season. O'Brien went on to score 56 goals in 125 games for City including both strikes in a 2-0 win over Blackpool in the club's first League game before leaving to end his career with Swindon Town.

OLDEST PLAYER

The oldest player to line-up in a Bristol City first team is Terry Cooper. He was 40 years 86 days old when he played his last game for the club against York City (Away 2-0) on 6 October 1984.

OSMAN, RUSSELL

Russell Osman began his Football League career with Ipswich Town where under the managership of Bobby Robson, he formed an excellent central defensive partnership with Terry Butcher. In 1975 he won an FA Youth Cup winners' medal though he had to wait until September 1977 before making his league debut against Chelsea.

Russell Osman

In May 1980 he won the first of 11 full international caps for England when he played against Australia. He twice went close to a League Championship medal as Town finished runners-up in the First Division in 1980-81 and 1981-82. He also helped Ipswich win the UEFA Cup in 1981 when they beat AZ67 Alkmaar 5-4 on aggregate. He had played in 384 games for the Suffolk club when he left Portman Road to join Leicester City for £240,000. He made 120 appearances for the Filbert Street club before signing for Southampton in June 1988.

Osman joined Bristol City in October 1991, manager Jimmy Lumsden paying £60,000 for his services. He made his debut for the Robins in a 1-0 home win over Watford and was an important member of the side for the next two seasons. Following the departure of Denis Smith, Osman became the club's player-manager and in 1993-94 plotted the FA Cup downfall of Liverpool. He had scored three goals in 83 games for the Robins when he was dismissed in November 1994.

After spells with Plymouth Argyle, Sudbury Town and Brighton, Osman became manager of Cardiff City but lost his job, being replaced by Frank Burrows.

OVERSEAS PLAYERS

There has been quite an influx of overseas players at Ashton Gate since the signing of Dutch international winger Geert Meijer and Finnish international Perti Jantunen. Neijer joined City from Ajax for £80,000 whilst Jantunen cost £50,000 from Eskilstuna, both arriving at Ashton Gate in March 1979. Unfortunately neither player reproduced their best form during their short stay with the club. Tall Swedish international goalkeeper Jan Moller followed manager Bob Houghton to Ashton Gate from Malmo, having played in the 1977 European Cup Final for the Swedish champions when they were beaten by Nottingham Forest. He made 48 appearances before following Houghton to Toronto Blizard. Versatile Dutch midfielder Ray Atteveld joined the Robins from Everton in March 1992 for a fee of £250,000. His stay at Ashton Gate was marred by a series of injuries and disciplinary problems. One of the most popular overseas players to turn out for the Robins was Polish international Jackie Dziekanowski. He arrived at Ashton Gate from Celtic for a fee of £250,000 and went on to score nine goals in 53 first team outings before rejoining one of his former clubs, Legia Warsaw.

Norwegian defender Vegard Hansen joined City from Stromsgodset in November 1994 and spent two seasons at Ashton Gate before returning to his homeland.

Australian internationals David Seal and Paul Agostino were joint top scorers for the Robins in 1995-96 but after helping the club to the play-offs the following season, both strikers left the club.

Sieb Dykstra, the colourful Dutch goalkeeper had a loan spell at Ashton Gate before rejoining Queen's Park Rangers whilst Bermudan international Shaun Goater scored 43 goals in 93 games before joining Manchester City for £400,000 in March 1998.

Recent overseas players to play for Bristol City include Danish international striker Soren Andersen and Danish Under-21 'keeper Bo Andersen, Hungarian international defender Vilmos Sebok, Moldovian Ivan Testimitanu, Dutch defender Clemens Zwijnenberg, Italian striker Lorenzo Pinamonte and Canadian international Jim Brennan.

OWERS, GARY

Versatile midfielder Gary Owers began his career with Sunderland, playing his first game in the Wearsider's colours in a 1-0 win at Brentford on the opening day of the 1987-88 season. After that, the combative midfield player was a virtual ever-present for the next eight seasons, appearing in 320 first team games and scoring 27 goals. At the end of his first season, he had won a Third Division Championship medal and in 1989-90 helped the club win promotion to the First Division after Swindon Town, who had beaten the Wearsiders in the play-off final were relegated to the Second Division after the discovery of financial irregularities at the County Ground club.

Owers left Roker Park in December 1994, joining Bristol City as part of the £450,000 exchange deal that took Martin Scott to the north-east. He made his City debut in a 1-0 defeat at West Bromwich Albion on Boxing Day. After suffering with injuries and a loss of form at Ashton Gate, he had a great 1996-97 season. An ever-present, he captained the Robins to the play-off semi-final where they lost to Brentford and scored many crucial goals throughout the campaign. Owers had scored 12 goals in 153 games when in the summer of 1998 he was allowed to leave and join Notts County.

OWN GOALS
Though a number of City players have had the misfortune to score an own goal, the only one to do so on his first team debut was popular full-back Trevor Jacobs. He did so on 26 November 1966 as the Robins drew 3-3 at Rotherham United.

P

PALMER, JOE
Army sergeant Joe Palmer became Bristol City's first team trainer soon after the appointment of George Hedley as manager. A strong disciplinarian, he demanded that players under his control should be dedicated and very fit. When League football resumed in 1919, Palmer was appointed as the club's trainer-manager.

He took the Robins to an FA Cup semi-final in 1920 where they lost to Huddersfield Town and to third place in Division Two in 1920-21, thus just missing promotion. Things began to go wrong at the start of the following season and after a series of disagreements with the directors, he resigned.

After a spell as trainer at Bradford Park Avenue, he took over as manager of Bristol Rovers.

A three-year spell with the then Eastville club ended with his dismissal in May 1929 after Rovers' second successive season in the bottom four of the Third Division.

PARR, GORDON
The captain of Bristol Boys and an England Schools triallist, he joined City in February 1957. After impressing in the club's reserve side, the uncompromising defender made his league debut in a goalless home draw against Middlesbrough at the end of the year. Though he played in another game towards the end of that 1957-58 season, it was September 1962 before he represented the first team again. This was partly due to him being absent on National Service in the Royal Air Force. After establishing himself as a first team regular, he helped the Robins to win promotion to the Second Division in 1964-65. Parr was also a member of the City side that reached the fifth round of the FA Cup in seasons 1966-67 and 1967-68 and the League Cup semi-finals in 1970-71.

Parr, who went on to score four goals in 332 games for the Ashton Gate club, was given a free transfer by manager Alan Dicks and left the club in the summer of 1972 to play for Irish League champions, Waterford. After playing in the European Cup for the Irish side, he later returned to the south-west to see out his career with non-League Minehead Town.

PAUL, JOHNNY

Johnny Paul joined Bristol City from Port Glasgow in August 1922 and made his debut two months later in a 3-0 win at Southend United. That season the Robins won the Third Division (South) Championship, Paul scoring his first goal for the club in a 3-1 home win over Charlton Athletic on the final day of the campaign, in what was his sixth appearance.

Over the next seven seasons, he partnered players such as Albert Fairclough and Tot Walsh, having his best campaign in terms of goals scored in 1926-27. That season he had scored 12 goals in the first 18 games including a hat-trick in a 4-2 win over Plymouth Argyle, when injury forced him to miss the rest of a campaign which saw the club once again win the Third Division (South) title.

He was never quite as prolific on his return but scored 51 goals in 215 League and Cup games before leaving Ashton Gate in November 1930 to play non-League football for Taunton Town. Sadly a serious knee injury ended his career soon after.

PEACOCK, ERNIE

Ernie 'Ginger' Peacock began his career with Notts County during the Second World War, occasionally 'guesting' for Bath City. The fiery wing-half left Meadow Lane in October 1946 to join his home-town club, Bristol City. He made a goalscoring debut for the Robins the following month but City were beaten 2-1 at home by Walsall. Peacock missed very few games over the next eleven seasons, being ever-present in 1952-53. When the club won the Third Division (South) Championship in 1954-55, Peacock, who missed just two games, was forced to switch to centre-half following the retirement of Dennis Roberts.

When City as a Second Division club reached the fifth round of the FA Cup in seasons 1956-57 and 1957-58, it was the tireless performances of Ernie Peacock that were a key factor in the Robins' progress. Peacock, who scored seven goals in 366 games for the Ashton Gate club, left City in the summer of 1959 to play for Weymouth Town. He later had a spell as player-manager of Taunton Town before ending his involvement with the game to become a car salesman. Sadly, heart trouble led to his premature death in February 1973 at the age of 49.

PEARCE, JIM

Former Welsh amateur centre-half Jim Pearce played his early football for his home-town team, Chirk. He had also represented the Royal Tank Corps before Bristol City manager Bob Hewison secured his services in the summer of 1934.

Pearce made his City debut in a 1-0 home win over Reading early the following season and held his place in the side for the next five seasons. In 1934-35 he was instrumental in the Third Division (South) club reaching the fifth round of the FA Cup, having an outstanding game in the goalless home draw against First Division Preston North End.

He went on to score two goals in 162 League and Cup games before leaving to play for Rochdale in May 1939.

His league career halted by the Second World War, Pearce turned his attention to the British Army whom he represented during wartime service in Greece and the Middle East.

PENALTIES

The club's first-ever goal from the penalty-spot in the Football League was scored by Richard Davies in a 2-1 home win over Leicester Fosse on 9 November 1901. The last City player to score from the spot at the time of writing was Mickey Bell who scored the opening goal in the 2-0 win over Sheffield United on 5 December 1998.

When City won the Second Division Championship in 1905-06, eight of their goals came from the penalty-spot and all were scored by Walter Bennett. This total was equalled by Tom Ritchie in 1983-84 who four seasons earlier had scored from the spot in the first three matches of City's last season in the top flight. However, in 1923-24 Sandy Torrance scored in four consecutive appearances for the club but only one of these games was won.

City goalkeeper Tony Cook saved a penalty on his debut as the Robins beat Swindon Town 4-2 on 8 November 1952.

PENALTY SHOOT-OUTS

After beating Bolton Wanderers 3-0 in 1985-86 to win the Freight Rover Trophy at Wembley, City won through to the final again the following season where they faced Mansfield Town. A record crowd of 55,586 saw the Stags deservedly take the lead and it was completely against the run of play when Glyn Riley equalised in the closing minutes of the game. There were no further goals in extra-time and so for the first time, a Wembley final went to a penalty shoot-out which Mansfield won after Gordon Owen had missed his kick for the Robins.

PETERS, FRANK

Outside-right Frank Peters played his early football for Wellington St George where his performances led to Coventry City securing his services in 1929. However, he was unable to win a first team spot and a year later, he left Highfield Road and joined Charlton Athletic. After one game for Fulham in which he scored a spectacular goal at Norwich, Peters joined Swindon Town in July 1933.

In three seasons at the County Ground, Peters scored 44 goals and it was this form that attracted Bristol City manager Bob Hewison. Peters joined the Robins in May 1936 and made his debut in the opening game of the 1936-37 season, a 3-2 home win over Queen's Park Rangers. When City finished runners-up in the Third Division (South) in 1937-38, it was Peters who provided the crosses from which Alfie Rowles scored many of his 18 goals. Frank Peters scored 22 goals in 118 League and Cup games prior to the outbreak of the Second World War when he hung up his boots.

PETERS, ROGER

Bearing more than a passing resemblance to Lou Costello of the famous comedy duo of Abbott and Costello, the Cheltenham-born speedy winger was given the nickname 'Lou'. A former England Youth international, he made his City debut in the last match of the 1960-61 season as John Ateyo scored a hat-trick in a 3-0 home win over Brentford. Though he made a number of appearances for the club over the next three seasons, it was 1964-65 when City won promotion from the Third Division as runners-up to Carlisle United, that Peters established a regular place. The following season in Division Two, Peters was in outstanding form as the club mounted a serious challenge for promotion to the top flight. Though not a prolific scorer, he topped the club's scoring charts in 1966-67 with 12 goals in all competitions. He had scored 28 goals in 180 games for the Robins when he was allowed to leave Ashton Gate in the summer of 1968 and join Bournemouth who paid £5,000 for his services.

Unable to settle at Dean Court, he later played non-League football for Bath City before hanging up his boots to work for Sun Life Insurance Company.

PITCH
The Ashton Gate pitch measures 115 yards by 75 yards.

PLASTIC
Four Football League clubs replaced their normal grass playing pitches with artificial surfaces at one stage or another. Queen's Park Rangers were the first in 1981 but the Loftus Road plastic was discarded in 1985 in favour of a return to turf. Luton Town (1985) Oldham Athletic (1986) and Preston North End (1986) followed. The Robins never played on the Kenilworth Road plastic which is perhaps just as well following their results at the other three venues.

City lost 3-0 at Queen's Park Rangers in the 1981-82 League Cup competition and 2-1 at Oldham Athletic in 1990-91. The club played three times on the Deepdale plastic and after two 2-0 defeats, secured a point in a 2-2 draw in 1989-90.

PLAYER OF THE YEAR
The Bristol City Supporters Club Player of the Year award has gone to the following players:

1970-71	Gerry Sharpe	1985-86	Bobby Hutchinson
1971-72	Geoff Merrick	1986-87	Rob Newman
1972-73	John Emanuel	1987-88	Alan Walsh
1973-74	Gerry Gow	1988-89	Keith Waugh
1974-75	Gary Collier	1989-90	Bob Taylor
1975-76	The Whole Team	1990-91	Andy Llewellyn
1976-77	Norman Hunter	1991-92	Martin Scott
1977-78	Norman Hunter	1992-93	Keith Welch
1978-79	Gerry Gow	1993-94	Wayne Allison
1979-80	Geoff Merrick	1994-95	Matt Bryant
1980-81	Kevin Mabbutt	1995-96	Martin Kuhl
1981-82	No Award	1996-97	Shaun Taylor
1982-83	Glyn Riley	1997-98	Shaun Taylor
1983-84	Howard Pritchard	1998-99	Ade Akinbiyi
1984-85	Alan Walsh	1999-00	Billy Mercer

PLAY-OFFS

Bristol City were first involved in the play-offs in 1987-88 after they had finished fifth in the Third Division. In the two-legged semi-final, City faced Second Division Sheffield United and in front of a 25,335 crowd at Ashton Gate won 1-0 courtesy of an Alan Walsh goal. In a difficult return leg, Carl Shutt extended City's lead before the Blades pulled a goal back. Keith Waugh made a number of fine saves and the Robins won through to the final 2-1 on aggregate. In the first leg of the final against Walsall at Ashton Gate, City were well beaten 3-1 and so had a mountain to climb in the return leg at Fellows Park. Against all the odds, goals from Newman and Shutt gave City a 2-0 win and so a third match was necessary. After losing a penalty shoot-out, City had to travel to Fellows Park again, but this time were well beaten by Walsall 4-0, for whom David Kelly scored a hat-trick.

City were involved in the play-offs again in 1996-97 after a late run saw them finish fifth in Division Two. The first leg of the semi-final against Brentford was shown live on Sky Sports and was no doubt responsible for the disappointingly low crowd of 15,581. The Bees won 2-1 with Gordon Owers scoring City's goal. In the second leg at Griffin Park, Darren Barnard levelled the scores on aggregate but Brentford scored two late goals to win 4-2 on aggregate.

POCOCK, BILL

Impressive performances for Bedminster St Francis and in Army soccer led to City manager Joe Palmer signing the fast-raiding left winger in August 1919. He played his first game for the club in a 1-0 home win over Bury on the opening day of the 1919-20 season. That campaign, Pocock, who scored 10 goals in 39 games, was instrumental in the club reaching the FA Cup semi-finals where they lost 2-1 to Huddersfield Town. The following season he played many of his games at inside-forward, forming an effective striking partnership with Jonah Wilcox, both of them ending the campaign as joint-top scorer with 14 goals.

After that, Pocock reverted to his position on the wing and created numerous goalscoring opportunities for the likes of Fairclough and Tot Walsh, helping the club win the Third Division (South) Championship in 1922-23.

He had scored 47 goals in 255 games for City when he left Ashton Gate in the summer of 1926. He later returned to live in the area, becoming head groundsman at Bedminster Down Sports Ground.

POINTS

Under the three points for a win system which was introduced in 1981-82, Bristol City's best points tally was the 91 points in 1989-90 when the club were runners-up to Bristol Rovers in the Third Division. However, the club's best points haul under the old two points for a win system was 70 points in 1954-55 when City won the Third Division (South) Championship.

City's worst record under either system was the meagre 23 points secured in 1931-32 when the club finished bottom of the Second Division and were relegated.

POSTPONED

The bleak winter of 1962-63, described at the time as the 'Modern Ice Age' proved to be one of the most chaotic seasons in British soccer. The worst Saturday for League action in that awful winter was 9 February when only seven Football League fixtures went ahead. The worst Saturday for the FA Cup was 5 January, the day of the third round, when only three of the 32 ties could be played and we first saw the introduction of the Pools Panel. City drew a twice-postponed third round tie against Aston Villa on 16 January but were then nine more postponements before the Robins lost 3-2 in the replay at Villa Park.

PRITCHARD, HOWARD

Welsh international winger Howard Pritchard joined Bristol City as an apprentice in the summer of 1976, later signing professional forms for the Ashton Gate club. His first game in City's colours was in an Anglo-Scottish Cup tie against Partick Thistle at Firhill which City lost 2-0 but he had to wait until the visit of Aston Villa on 26 August 1978 before making his Football League debut. Over the next three seasons, Pritchard was in and out of the City team and in August 1981 he was allowed to join Swindon Town on a free transfer.

In two years at the County Ground, the Cardiff-born player scored 11 goals in 65 league games, prompting City manager Terry Cooper to bring him back to Ashton Gate for a second spell. He was ever-present in 1983-84 when the club finished fourth in Division Four, scoring 10 goals. When the Robins won the Freight Rover Trophy in 1986, Pritchard, who had been capped at full international level by Wales against Norway, scored one of the goals in the 3-0 win over Bolton Wanderers.

He went on to score 29 goals in 182 League and Cup games for City before joining Gillingham for a fee of £22,500 in August 1986. After two seasons at the Priestfield Stadium he moved on to play for Walsall, Maidstone United and finally Yeovil Town.

PROMOTION

Bristol City have been promoted on nine occasions. The first occasion was in 1905-06 when the club won the Second Division Championship. They suffered only two defeats in 38 matches, winning 30 and drawing six of their other games. Thirty-one of their points came from away matches and during the course of the season, they won 14 consecutive league matches. The club's second experience of promotion came in 1922-23 when after just one season of playing in the Third Division (South), City won the Championship, finishing six points ahead of runners-up Plymouth Argyle. However, the Robins were relegated after just one season in the Second Division and this time spent three seasons in the Third Division (South) before winning the Championship again, finishing two points clear of rivals Plymouth Argyle. In fact, the Devon club finished runners-up in the Third Division (South) for six consecutive seasons!

Relegated in 1931-32, City spent 16 seasons either side of the Second World War playing in the Third Division (South) before winning promotion in 1954-55. They started the season in grand style, being unbeaten in their first 13 matches and equalling the Division's record for both points (70) - nine ahead of Leyton Orient - and wins (30) set by Nottingham Forest four years earlier. Of their 101 goals, John Ateyo scored 28 and Jimmy Rogers 25.

City won promotion again in 1964-65 when they clinched the second promotion place in the Third Division with a slightly better goal average than Mansfield Town, whom they had failed to beat in their two league meetings. The club won promotion for a sixth time in 1975-76 when despite suffering two unexpected defeats at the hands of Blackpool (Away 1-2) and Notts County (Home 1-2) they beat Portsmouth (Home 1-0) to clinch second place in Division Two.

Following three successive relegation seasons, the Robins won promotion from the Fourth Division in 1983-84, finishing fourth behind champions York City, Doncaster Rovers and Reading. After six seasons of Third Division football, City won promotion in 1989-90. Their total of 91 points would normally have been enough to clinch the Championship but they had to settle for runners-up spot behind Bristol Rovers of all teams!

The club's last experience of promotion came in 1997-98 when the Robins finished runners-up in the Second Division, three points behind Watford.

PULIS, TONY

A former Welsh Youth international, Tony Pulis was a cool and polished defender who played most of his football around the lower divisions. He started with Bristol Rovers before joining Newport County but it was with Bournemouth that he enjoyed his greatest success, helping the Cherries win the Third Division Championship in 1986-87. After a spell as assistant-manager to Harry Redknapp at Dean Court, he was appointed his successor when Harry moved to West Ham United as Billy Bond's assistant. Pulis left Bournemouth in 1994 and the following year took charge at Gillingham. His first season at the Priestfield Stadium was a huge success as the Gills won promotion to Division Two.

In July 1999, Tony Pulis was appointed manager of Bristol City but after just six months in charge he left Ashton Gate to take over the reins at Portsmouth.

Q

QUICKEST GOAL
The quickest goal in the history of Bristol City was scored by John Ateyo after just nine seconds in the 2-0 home win over Bury on 16 March 1957.

QUIGLEY, JOHNNY
Glasgow-born Johnny Quigley began his footballing career with Celtic before being released. He joined Nottingham Forest in July 1957 from Ashfield Juniors and made his League debut three months later, scoring the winner in a 4-3 defeat of Spurs at White Hart Lane. On 8 November 1958 he became the first Forest player to score a post-war First Division hat-trick as the Reds beat Manchester City 4-0. He was the scorer of some vital goals for Forest, perhaps none more so than the one against Aston Villa at Hillsborough in the FA Cup semi-final of 1959. After scoring 58 goals in 270 games, he left the City Ground to join Huddersfield Town.

From there he moved to Bristol City as part of the deal which saw Brian Clark join the Yorkshire club. After a disappointing debut game at Northampton, which City lost 2-1, Quigley was appointed club captain. He was a great favourite with the Ashton Gate crowd but after scoring seven goals in 78 games he was surprisingly sold to Mansfield Town for £3,000 in July 1968.

He inspired the Stags to two superb FA Cup runs but after becoming assistant-manager to Jock Basford at Field Mill, he was dismissed in November 1971 and went to coach in the Middle East.

R

RAISBECK, ALEX

Alex Raisbeck was a superb centre-half who won two League Championship medals with Liverpool around the turn of the century. He played for several junior clubs before joining Hibernian in 1896 and at 18 years of age, he played for the Scottish League against the Irish League.

In March 1898 he came south of the border to play for Stoke where his outstanding performances attracted the attention of Liverpool. After joining the Reds for a fee of £350 in May 1898, Raisbeck went on to score 21 goals in 340 League and Cup games for the Anfield club. His League Championship medals came in 1900-01 and 1905-06 and a Second Division Championship medal in 1904-05. He was capped eight times by his country and has to go down as the first of a number of outstanding Scots to influence the course of the Anfield club's history.

In 1909, Raisbeck returned to Scotland to join Partick Thistle for a £500 fee. In 1914 he became secretary-manager of Hamilton Academical, until 1917 when he became a director of the club.

In December 1921, Raisbeck was appointed manager of Bristol City. Though he came too late to save the club from relegation from the Second Division, he led the Robins to the Third Division (South) Championship in 1922-23. Unfortunately they finished bottom of the Second Division the following season when they suffered their heaviest home defeat, losing 8-0 to Derby County. After signing Tot Walsh from Bolton Wanderers and Walter Wadsworth from Liverpool, City finished third in 1924-25 and fourth in 1925-26 before winning the Third Division (South) title again in 1926-27. Raisbeck resigned his post as Bristol City manager in June 1929 after the club had narrowly avoided relegation from the Second Division.

On leaving Ashton Gate, Raisbeck managed Halifax Town and in 1934-35 led the Yorkshire club to runners-up in the Third Division (North). After a spell managing Chester, Raisbeck took charge of non-League Bath City before returning to his beloved Liverpool to work as a scout.

RECEIPTS

The club's record receipts are £148,282 for the FA Cup fourth round match against Everton at Ashton Gate on 29 January 1995.

RELEGATION

Bristol City have suffered the experience of relegation on ten occasions. The first was 1910-11 when the club finished 19th in Division One and lost their place in the top flight after winning promotion five seasons earlier. During the 1920s, the club were relegated twice - 1921-22 and 1923-24, whilst the period also saw them win the Third Division (South) Championship on two occasions. The club's fourth experience of relegation came in 1931-32 when they finished bottom of the Second Division with just 23 points secured from their 42 matches. After 16 seasons of playing in the Third Division (South) City won promotion in 1954-55 only to be relegated again in 1959-60, when following a dismal campaign in which they were one of the promotion favourites, they finished bottom of Division Two with 27 points. Having won promotion to the Second Division in 1964-65, the Robins finished runners-up to Sunderland in 1975-76 to win promotion to the top flight.

They lost their First Division status in 1979-80 after finishing third from bottom, despite a reasonable start to the campaign.

The relegation of Bristol City and Bristol Rovers from Division Two at the end of the following season was the first time two teams from the same provincial town or city had gone down in the same season since Bradford City and Bradford Park Avenue were relegated from the First and Second Division respectively in 1921-22. City finished 23rd in the Third Division in 1981-82 and by 4 December 1982, they were 92nd in the League as bottom club in the Fourth Division.

City's ninth experience of relegation came in 1994-95 when despite the re-appointment of Joe Jordan as manager, the Robins finished 23rd in the First Division. The club were last relegated in 1998-99 when they finished bottom of Division One, five points behind Port Vale who finished just outside the relegation zone.

RENNIE, DAVID

The winner of 20 Scottish Youth caps, David Rennie played in Scotland's UEFA Youth championship-winning team of 1982. He joined Leicester City straight from school but spent most of his time at Filbert Street in the reserves until his £50,000 transfer to Leeds United in January 1986.

He went on to play in 115 games for the Elland Road club before Howard Wilkinson sold him to Bristol City for £200,000 in August 1989.

He was an important member of the Robins' side that won promotion to the Second Division in 1989-90, just missing one game. One of his best games for the club came in the third round FA Cup match with Wimbledon in 1991-92 which ended all-square at 1-1 before an Andy May goal gave City victory in the replay at Plough Lane. He went on to score eight goals in 126 games for the Ashton Gate club before moving to Birmingham City in February 1992.

After helping the Blues win promotion that season, Terry Cooper swapped him from Coventry City winger David Smith in April 1993. He went on to skipper the Sky Blues in the Premiership but sadly suffered badly from injuries during his time at Highfield Road. He had made 92 appearances for Coventry before being released during the 1996 close season and joining Northampton Town. After a good start he lost his place to David Brightwell and moved to Peterborough United where his season was disrupted due to a hernia operation.

RILEY, GLYN

Glyn Riley began his Football League career with Barnsley, helping the Oakwell club rise from the Fourth Division to the Second in the space of three seasons. He had scored 16 goals in 130 games when following a loan spell with Doncaster Rovers, Terry Cooper brought him to Ashton Gate on a free transfer.

He made his City debut on the opening day of the 1982-83 season, scoring the winning goal in a 2-1 defeat of Hull City. He ended that season as the club's leading scorer with 16 goals, a total that included a hat-trick in a 4-2 home win over Wimbledon. Voted the club's Player of the Year in 1982-83, he formed a prolific goalscoring partnership with Alan Walsh and topped the club's scoring charts again the following season.

He helped City win the Freight Rover Trophy in 1986, scoring twice in the final as the Robins beat Bolton Wanderers 3-0 in front of a Wembley crowd of 54,502. Riley went on to score 69 goals in 226 League and Cup games for City before following a loan spell with Torquay United, he joined Aldershot for

David Rennie

£15,000 in October 1987.

He later played non-League football for Bath City, helping them regain Conference status in 1989-90.

RILEY, JOE

After playing his early football with Denaby United and Goldthorpe United, Joe Riley joined Bristol Rovers and was the first player for the Eastville club to score a hat-trick on his debut. Despite this start, he was unable to hold down a first team place with Rovers due to the fine form of England internationals Tommy Cook and Viv Gibbins. Riley left Eastville in the summer of 1933.

He made his League debut for the Robins in a 3-0 home defeat at the hands of his former club on the opening day of the 1933-34 season but soon discovered his shooting boots and ended the campaign as the club's leading scorer. He scored all five goals in the 5-0 home win over Brighton and Hove Albion in February 1934 and two of City's goals in the 3-0 Welsh Cup final replay win over Tranmere Rovers.

He had scored 26 goals in 77 games for City when he left to join Bournemouth. In two seasons at Dean Court, he was the Cherries' leading scorer. He later played for Notts County before returning to Ashton Gate as City's scout.

RIPPON, WILLIS

Willis Rippon had played junior football for several Sheffield youth sides before joining Bristol City. He made his debut for the Robins in a 2-1 home win over Manchester City in October 1907 though it was the following season before he won a regular place in the Ashton Gate club's side. That campaign saw him score five goals in the club's run to the FA Cup Final including penalties in each of the two matches against Derby County at the semi-final stage. He started the 1909-10 season in fine style but injuries restricted his appearances and in July 1910 after scoring 19 goals in 46 games he was transferred to Woolwich Arsenal.

After scoring in each of his first two league games of which his debut was against Manchester United, he lost his place to newly signed John Chalmers and dissatisfied with reserve team football, moved to Brentford. He later played for Hamilton Academicals, Grimsby Town and Rotherham Town.

RITCHIE, TOM

Edinburgh-born striker Tom Ritchie began his career with Bridgend Thistle and it was from here that Bristol City manager Alan Dicks signed him in the summer of 1969. After a number of impressive performances for the club's reserve side, Ritchie was given his league debut in the second game of the 1972-73 season, a 2-2 home draw with Millwall. After that, he missed very few games and in 1975-76 when the club won promotion to the First Division, Ritchie, who was ever-present, was also City's leading scorer. His total of 18 goals included a hat-trick in a 4-1 win over York City. He was hampered by injuries during the club's first season in the top flight but then topped City's goalscoring charts for the next three seasons. During that time, he helped the Robins win the Anglo-Scottish Cup in 1977-78, netting a hat-trick in the 3-1 defeat of Bristol Rovers.

Following City's relegation in 1979-80, Ritchie left Ashton Gate and joined Sunderland for a fee of £180,000. Despite helping to keep the Wearsiders in the First Division, he couldn't win a regular place and after a loan spell with Carlisle United, Ritchie, who had scored 11 goals in 40 games for Sunderland returned to Ashton Gate on a free transfer.

He had two more outstanding seasons, taking his tally of goals to 113 in 468 League and Cup games before surprisingly being allowed to leave and join Yeovil Town, where he teamed up with Gerry Gow.

ROBERTS, DENNIS

Dennis Roberts was a commanding centre-half who began his career as an amateur with Huddersfield Town. In August 1937 he joined Notts County but unable to win a regular first team place, he moved to Bristol City on a free transfer a year later. Roberts played his first game for the Robins in a 1-1 draw at Clapton Orient in September 1938. He was a regular in the City side throughout the Second World War, appearing in 205 wartime games.

When League football resumed in 1946-47, Roberts was still the club's first-choice centre-half and though he never won any honours during his time at Ashton Gate he did play in 331 League and Cup games for the club. His two league goals came in the 1-1 draw against Plymouth Argyle on Boxing Day 1951 and the 4-3 defeat by Newport County in September 1952.

The season after Roberts played his last game for the club, City won the Third Division (South) Championship!

RODGERS, ARNOLD

An ex-miner from Wickersley near Rotherham, Arnold Rodgers began his career as a left-half but on joining Huddersfield Town in March 1942, he was converted to a centre-forward. Though never a regular with the Terriers, he had scored 17 goals in 28 games in the First Division for the Yorkshire club when Bob Wright stepped in to sign him for £5,000 in October 1949.

Rodgers made his Bristol City debut at Notts County, netting the Robins' goal in a 4-1 defeat. He ended his first season at the club as City's top-scorer with 18 goals in 28 games. In fact, Rodgers was the club's leading marksman in each of his first four seasons at Ashton Gate with a best of 26 in 33 games in 1952-53. That total included his first hat-trick for the club in a 5-1 home win over Watford.

Forming a prolific goalscoring partnership with John Ateyo, he continued to find the net on a regular basis and in September 1954 he netted another hat-trick in a 4-0 defeat of Colchester United. That season, City won promotion as champions of the Third Division (South) but early the next campaign, Rodgers, who had scored 111 goals in 204 League and Cup games, left to play for Shrewsbury Town.

After just one season at Gay Meadow he returned to Bristol to concentrate on his flower business, later managing Welton Rovers when they won three successive Western League Championships. He ended his involvement with the game after a spell managing Bath City.

RODGERS, DAVID

Former England Schoolboy international David Rodgers, the son of Arnold Rodgers, made a goalscoring debut for the Robins as they beat Leicester City 2-1 in a League Cup fourth round replay in November 1970. It was 1972-73 before he established himself fully in the City side, partnering Geoff Merrick, he helped the club finish fifth in Division Two. He was in outstanding form the following season as City reached the sixth round of the FA Cup only to be beaten 1-0 by Liverpool.

Losing his place to Gary Collier, Rodgers appeared in only 21 league games over the next three seasons, but returned to first team action in the club's second campaign in the First Division. He went on to score 18 goals in 227 League and Cup games before leaving to join Torquay United after the 'Ashton Gate Eight' crisis forced his release.

After a handful of league appearances for the Devon club, he ended his first-class career with Lincoln City before playing non-League football for Forest Green Rovers.

ROGERS, JIMMY

After joining Wolverhampton Wanderers from Rubery Owen FC, winger Jimmy Rogers found his first team opportunities at Molineux limited and in May 1950, City manager Bob Wright secured his services on a free transfer. During his time with Wolves, Rogers, who had to do National Service, represented the Combined Services.

He made his Bristol City debut in a 4-1 defeat at Torquay United and though he held his place for the next game at Swindon, it was 1951-52 before he won a regular spot. Forming a good understanding with John Ateyo, he helped the club win the Third Division (South) Championship in 1954-55, scoring 25 goals in 44 games. The following season in Division Two, Rogers netted 25 goals in 34 games, a total that included hat-tricks in the wins over Plymouth Argyle (Home 6-0) and Doncaster Rovers (Home 4-1).

In December 1956 he moved to Coventry City with Jack Boxley and in 1958-59 helped the Highfield Road club win promotion to the Third Division. After scoring 27 goals in 76 games for the Midlands club he returned to Ashton Gate for a second spell. He had taken his tally of goals to 108 in 287 League and Cup games when he left to become player-manager of Cinderford Town.

ROWLES, ALF

After a series of impressive goalscoring performances for Weston-super-Mare in the Somerset League, Alf Rowles was invited to Ashton Gate to take part in a trial.

Rowles made his Bristol City debut against Exeter City on 15 January 1938, scoring a hat-trick in a 4-1 win. Rowles scored in each of his next five league games, netting another hat-trick in the last game of this sequence as Walsall were beaten 8-2 at Fellows Park. Though he only played in 14 games in that season of 1937-38, he scored 18 goals to help the club finish runners-up in the Third Division (South). Early the following season in the match against Notts County which City won 2-1, Rowles collided with the visiting 'keeper, his damaged knee virtually ending his playing career. Rowles, who had scored 20 goals in 24 games was forced to give up the game on medical grounds.

He returned to work in his original trade as a fitter, whilst also acting as trainer to Bristol City's youth side.

ROYLE, JOE

Joe Royle became Everton's youngest player when on 15 January 1966 at the age of 16 years 288 days he played at Blackpool. It was 1967-68 before he could claim a regular first team spot and the following season he was the club's top scorer with 22 goals, a total which included a hat-trick in a 7-1 win over Leicester City.

Royle became a top-class target man, top-scoring for the Blues for the next three seasons. He netted another hat-trick in a 4-2 win over Southampton in September 1969 and four goals against the same opposition in November 1971 as the Saints were beaten 8-0. After being capped ten times for the England Under-23 side, he made his full international debut against Malta in February 1971.

He had scored 119 goals in 275 games for Everton when he was transferred to Manchester City in December 1974. He scored 31 goals in 117 games for the Maine Road club before moving to Bristol City for £90,000 in November 1977.

He netted four goals on his Robins' debut as Middlesbrough were beaten 4-1, helping the club stave off relegation with eight goals in 26 games. In 1978-79, City's best season in terms of league placings for 70 years, Royle missed just two games, netting a hat-trick in a 5-0 win over Coventry City on Boxing Day. He had scored 20 goals in 112 League and Cup games when he left Ashton Gate to join Norwich City. Sadly, his playing career came to a premature end at Carrow Road and he entered management with Oldham Athletic.

He helped the Latics win promotion from the Second Division and reach the League Cup Final and FA Cup semi-finals. In November 1994 he returned to Goodison Park as manager but after keeping the club in the Premiership, he quit by mutual consent following clashes with the chairman over transfer deals.

Now manager of Manchester City, he helped them reach the First Division via the play-offs in 1998-99.

Joe Royle

RUSSELL, JOHN

John Russell began his career with the Scottish junior side Glasgow Thistle. He was transferred to Leith Athletic and played for St Mirren between 1894 and 1896. He joined Woolwich Arsenal from the Love Street club in June 1896 and in his one season with the club took over the left-wing position from Frank McAvoy, making his League debut in a 3-0 home win over Burton. He eventually went on to play in 23 of the last 25 league games of the season but in the summer, was transferred to Bristol City.

He scored on his debut in a 7-4 home win over Wolverton in the Southern League and ended his first season at the club with 12 goals in 44 games, picking up a Western League Championship medal in the process. In each of his first two seasons with the club, they finished as runners-up in the Southern League. One of City's most trickiest wingers, he went on to score 36 goals in 110 League and Cup games before leaving to join Blackburn Rovers. He never appeared in the Ewood Park club's League side and sadly died in August 1905, aged 32.

S

SCOTT, MARTIN

Sheffield-born left-back Martin Scott began his career with Rotherham United, making his league debut for the Millers eight months before signing professional forms. After helping the Yorkshire club win the Fourth Division Championship in 1988-89, Scott, who had made 114 appearances, became United's most expensive sale when in December 1990, Jimmy Lumsden paid £200,000 to take him to Ashton Gate.

In 1991-92 his first full season with the club, he was ever-present and voted City's Player of the Year, helping the Robins reach the fifth round of the FA Cup. He went on to be a first team regular with City for three seasons but in December 1994 after scoring 15 goals in 191 games he signed for Sunderland in a £750,000 exchange deal involving Gary Owers.

With the Wearsiders, he won two First Division Championship medals in 1995-96 and 1998-99 but at the end of the latter season, after which he had scored 11 goals in 126 games he left to join Premiership newcomers Bradford City.

SECOND DIVISION

Bristol City have had ten spells in the Second Division. Following their admission to the Football League in 1901-02, City finished sixth in their first season of Second Division football but in 1905-06 after four seasons of coming close to promotion to the First Division, won the Championship. Their total of 66 points was four more than runners-up Manchester United. After five seasons in the top flight, City were relegated and in 1911-12 began their second spell in Division Two, a spell that was to last seven seasons before the club were relegated to the Third Division in 1921-22. After winning the Championship at the first attempt, the Robins returned to Division Two but were relegated at the end of the season. Promotion followed in 1926-27 and the following season,

City embarked on their fourth spell in the Second Division. After five seasons of struggle, City were relegated in 1931-32 and didn't return to the Second Division until 1955-56. This fifth spell also lasted five seasons before the club finished bottom in 1959-60 and were relegated to the Third Division. The club's sixth and longest spell of 11 seasons began in 1965-66 and culminated in them winning promotion to the First Division in 1975-76 as runners-up to Sunderland. After four seasons of top flight football, the Robins were relegated but spent just one season, 1980-81 in the Second Division on their way down to the League's basement. After a number of seasons languishing in the lower divisions, City returned to the Second Division in 1990-91, it becoming the 'new' Division One in 1992-93 following the introduction of the Premiership. City were relegated in 1994-95 and spent three seasons in the Second Division before winning promotion in 1997-98 as runners-up to Watford. Unfortunately after just one season back in Division One, City were relegated and in 1999-2000 began their tenth spell in the Second Division.

SEMI-FINALS
Up to the end of the 1998-99 season, Bristol City had been involved in two FA Cup semi-finals and two League Cup semi-finals. They have also reached that stage of the Anglo-Scottish Cup, the Freight Rover Trophy, the Welsh Cup and the Third Division (South) Cup.

SHAIL, MARK
Born in Sweden of English parents, he moved to England when he was four and on leaving school, joined Worcester City. Though he moved to Yeovil Town he continued his studies and gained a degree in Psychology and Sociology at Surrey University. He helped Yeovil win the Bob Lord Trophy in 1989-90 and three seasons later starred in the FA Cup defeats of Torquay United and Hereford United as the Somerset club reached the third round where they lost to Arsenal.

City manager Russell Osman paid £45,000 for his services in March 1993 and he made his debut in a 1-1 draw at Peterborough United.

Good in the air, the central defender has suffered with a series of injuries over the last few seasons but his comeback in 1998-99 brought about an immediate improvement in the heart of the City defence. Appointed captain, he has always given of his best and led by example. Now in his seventh season at Ashton Gate, he has scored five goals in 149 League and Cup games, a record he will hope to improve on providing there are no further injury problems.

SHARPE, GERRY

Former apprentice Gerry Sharpe made his Bristol City debut in a 2-1 home defeat by Carlisle United in October 1964, seven months after turning professional. He went on to score six goals in 13 games that season as the club won promotion to the Second Division. Over the next three seasons he found himself in and out of the City side but in 1968-69 after Alan Dicks converted him from an inside-forward to an outside-left, he became a first team regular.

In 1969-70 he was the club's leading league goalscorer with 10 but midway through the following season, a double compound leg fracture in the home defeat by Middlesbrough ended his playing career at the age of 25.

After being awarded a testimonial against Derby County in December 1973, he became City's youth coach, later having a brief spell as the club's acting manager in May 1982. Gerry Sharpe is now coaching in Canada.

SHAW, JOHN

Goalkeeper John Shaw began his career with Leeds United, for whom his only appearances were in European ties - and he was substituted in both. With United holding a 2-0 first leg lead in their first round UEFA Cup tie against Belgian side Lierse SK, manager Don Revie fielded a string of reserves in the return clash. Leeds lost 4-0 and Shaw was replaced by Gary Sprake during the game. Two years later the Scottish-born 'keeper figured in a dramatic match at Hibernian, keeping a clean sheet until he was injured.

Shaw joined Bristol City on a free transfer in May 1974 but had to wait over two years before making his league debut in a 1-0 home defeat by Birmingham City in October 1976. He kept his place for 102 consecutive league matches being ever-present in 1977-78, a season in which he helped the club win the Anglo-Scottish Cup. Despite losing his place to Ray Cashley, Shaw, who suffered severe hair loss through a nervous complaint, fought his way back to become the club's first-choice 'keeper again. He enjoyed another long run of 124 consecutive league games, being ever-present in seasons 1982-83 and 1983-84 when the club won promotion. He went on to play in 367 games for the Robins before joining Exeter City in the summer of 1985. He made 109 league appearances for the Grecians but in 1988 left to play non-League football for Gloucester City.

John Shaw

SHELTON, GARY
Given his first taste of League soccer with Walsall when only 16-years-old, Gary Shelton moved to Aston Villa in January 1978 but in four seasons at Villa Park he played in only 24 league games. Never getting the chance to establish himself he jumped at the chance of joining Sheffield Wednesday for £50,000 in March 1982. He not only made an immediate impact in the Wednesday midfield but scored some vital goals as the Owls won promotion to the First Division in 1983-84. The following season he missed just one game and was chosen

Gary Shelton

as the over-age representative and captain of the England Under-21 side against Finland. In 1985-86 he suffered a number of minor injuries and loss of form but bounced back the following season to something like his old self. However in the summer of 1987 he joined Oxford United, playing in 79 games for the U's before moving to Bristol City in part-exchange for Steve McLaren in the summer of 1989.

Shelton was an inspirational figure in the City side, helping them win promotion to the Second Division in his first season at Ashton Gate. Though he suffered with injuries in 1991-92, he added much-needed steel to the Robins side and was a first team regular for four seasons. He had scored 27 goals in 180 games when following a loan spell with Rochdale he joined Chester City as player-coach.

SHERPA VAN TROPHY

The competition for Associate Members of the Football League was first sponsored by Sherpa Van in the 1987-88 season. Bristol City's first match in the Sherpa Van Trophy saw them beat Swansea City 2-0 with goals from Walsh and Shutt. Despite losing 3-1 to Wolves in their other group game, City qualified for the knockout stages only to lose 1-0 at Aldershot in the first round.

In 1988-89 the Robins lost their first group match 1-0 at Bristol Rovers but then bounced back to win 2-0 at home to Exeter City. In the first round City had to travel to Molineux but lost 3-0 to Wolves, the holders of the trophy.

SINCLAIR, FINLAY

After playing junior football for Elderslie and Linthouse, full-back Finlay Sinclair joined Glasgow Rangers with whom he won a Glasgow Cup medal. In June 1896 he moved south of the border to play for Woolwich Arsenal. At the Manor Fold he blossomed as the club's first-choice left-back in 1896-97. He made his league debut at Hyde Road in the match against Manchester City on the opening day of the season. He had played in 26 of the 30 league games when he was surprisingly allowed to leave the club in the summer of 1897 to link up with Bristol City.

Though he only spent a brief time with the Robins, appearing in just 16 League and Cup games, he earned a reputation as one of the club's most fearless defenders. Though his appearances for City were restricted by injury, he always gave of his best when he did turn out for the club.

SKIRTON, ALAN

Alan Skirton joined Arsenal from his home-town club Bath City in January 1959 while he was still completing his National Service. Unfortunately not long after joining the club, he contracted pleurisy and pneumonia which kept him out of action for well over eighteen months. On making a full recovery, he established a regular place in the Arsenal side and in 1961-62, his second season in the team, was the club's leading scorer with 19 goals. Following the emergence of George Armstrong, Skirton, who had scored 54 goals in 154 League and Cup games for the Gunners, joined Blackpool for £30,000 in September 1966.

Alan Skirton

Skirton scored on his Blackpool debut - at Highbury of all places - and the next season saw the Seasiders back in Division Two with Skirton their second-highest scorer. He had scored 28 goals in 87 games when Blackpool manager Stan Mortesnen allowed Skirton to return to the West Country and he joined Bristol City for £15,000 in November 1968.

His first game for the Robins was in a 1-0 home defeat by Norwich City and though the club were continually struggling against relegation in his time at Ashton Gate, Skirton's skill and experience shone through. He had scored 18 goals in 93 games including the opening goal of the 1970-71 League Cup semi-final first-leg game against Spurs, when he was given a free transfer and joined Torquay United.

He later played for Durban City and Weymouth, where on hanging up his boots, he became assistant commercial manager. After a spell as commercial manager with Bath City, he left to take up a similar position with Yeovil Town.

SMAILES, ANDY

Andy Smailes began his career as an inside-forward with Blyth Spartans before joining Newcastle United for £300 in October 1919. He had scored 30 goals in 77 games for the Magpies when Sheffield Wednesday paid £1,500 for his services in October 1922.

A year later, Smailes left Hillsborough to join Bristol City in an exchange deal involving Billy Walker. Smailes made his debut for the Robins in a 1-0 home defeat by Fulham. That season he was the club's second top scorer with seven goals in 30 games as they ended the campaign bottom of the Second Division. When City finished third in Division Three (South) in 1924-25, Smailes was the club's only ever-present. He continued to be a first team regular for the next four seasons, helping the club win the Third Division (South) Championship in 1926-27. He had scored 15 goals in 169 League and Cup games when he left Ashton Gate to play for Rotherham United in August 1929.

Smailes spent 18 years at Millmoor as the Yorkshire club's trainer before succeeding Reg Freeman as manager. In 1952-53 the Millers beat FA Cup holders Newcastle United 3-1 in the fourth round but in November 1958 with Rotherham bottom of their division, Smailes resigned, thus ending nearly thirty years with the club. He later managed Scarborough for two years.

SMALLEST PLAYER

Although such statistics are always unreliable for those playing before the turn of the twentieth century, it appears that the distinction of being Bristol City's smallest player goes to Billy Wedlock.

Standing just 5ft 4 ins, he was one of the best centre-halves to win international honours for England. The club's most capped international, the diminutive Wedlock won 26 caps for his country.

SMITH, DENNIS

Idolised by the Stoke public for his total commitment, he overcame countless injuries and broken bones to establish himself in the number five shirt which he was to make his own. After making his Potters' debut against Arsenal at Highbury in September 1968 he won a regular place alongside Alan Bloor at the heart of the Stoke defence. Not the most cultured of defenders, there were nonetheless not too many strikers who enjoyed playing against him. Though he represented the Football League, a full international cap eluded him. However, he won a winners' medal in 1972 as the Potters won the League Cup. Towards the end of his playing career, he joined the Stoke coaching staff and earned a well-deserved testimonial from the club.

After leaving Stoke where he made 470 appearances, he embarked on a career in management with York City, taking the club to its first major trophy when they won the Fourth Division Championship in 1983-84.

Smith along with his assistant Viv Busby moved to Sunderland in 1987. They helped the Wearsiders clinch the Third Division title in their first season at the club and then made the Second Division play-offs in 1990. They lost to Swindon in the final but were promoted when the Wiltshire club were relegated after an illegal betting scandal. The club lasted just one season in the top flight and when they struggled in the Second Division, Smith was sacked.

In March 1992, Smith replaced Jimmy Lumsden as Bristol City manager. Despite record signings Ray Atteveld and Andy Cole arriving at Ashton Gate during his time in charge, the club struggled at the wrong end of the table and after just ten months in charge, he was dismissed. He then took charge at Oxford United but after master-minding the promotion success of 1995-96, left to manage West Bromwich Albion where he was later replaced by Brian Little.

Dennis Smith

SPEAR, ARTHUR
Arthur Spear made his Bristol City debut in a 1-0 win at Glossop in December 1904, a season in which he appeared in all three half-back positions as cover for Billy Jones, Jim Hosie and Peter Chambers. It was midway through the club's Second Division Championship-winning season of 1905-06 when Spear won a regular place in the side, scoring his only goal for the club in a 2-0 home win over Leeds City in April 1906. Injuries limited his appearances in 1906-07 as City finished runners-up in the First Division but he was back in the Robins' side the following season and in 1908-09 played his part in the club reaching the FA Cup Final.

Spear, who appeared in 151 games for City, had a joint benefit match with Archie Annan against Everton in April 1911.

SPONSORS
The club's present sponsors are the Bristol-based DAS Group, the leading legal expenses insurance company in the United Kingdom. Previous sponsors include Sanderson Computer Recruitment, Thorn Security, Hirerite, Autowindscreens and Dry Blackthorn Cider.

SOUTHERN LEAGUE
After being elected straight into the First Division at the end of the 1896-97 season, Bristol City changed their name from Bristol South End, adopted professionalism and became a limited company with a capital of £2,500. With all these changes it was decided to appoint a full-time manager and Sam Hollis was chosen. Prior to joining City he had been trainer/coach with Woolwich Arsenal and he was given the princely sum of £40 for new players. It was to his old club that he turned, signing four Gunners - Paddy O'Brien, Jock Russell, Alex Caie and Finlay Sinclair. Other signings included 'keeper Hugh Monteith and Billy Jones from Loughborough, Harry Davy and Albert Carnelly from Leicester Fosse and Billy Higgins from Grimsby Town. City in their first season became the undisputed kings of Bristol soccer over rivals Warmley, Eastville Rovers and St George's. City, who lost only two games were the league's top scorers and ended the campaign as runners-up to Southampton. In 1898-99 Southampton were champions for the third season running, just ahead of Bristol City. The Championship hinged on the final game of the season at the St John's Ground, Bristol on

29 April. City were unbeaten at home and led 2-0 at half-time. The Saints fought back and won a magnificent match 4-3 to clinch the title by a mere two points. Bedminster, who finished three places above City, who were ninth in 1899-1900, amalgamated with the Robins. Many saw it as an 'absorption' though it was Ashton Gate, Bedminster's home that was developed instead of City's St John's Lane. The clubs played within two miles of each other and with Rovers also playing in the city, it was inevitable that one club should fold.

City manager Bob Campbell now had a wealth of talent at his disposal. There were more players from Bedminster than City in the side for the 1900-01 season. However, success on the field was achieved only at a price. High wages and insufficient income brought the creditors calling as the Bristol club made a £974 loss on the year. Mr Hodgkinson the secretary saw the solution to the problem as the club leaving the Southern League, after finishing as runners-up again, to join the Football League. This was agreed by the board of directors and City were duly elected to the Second Division in the summer of 1901.

STANIFORTH, FRED

Fred Staniforth who played for both Kilnhurst Town and Rotherham Main, was turning out for Mexborough Town when Bristol City manager Harry Thickett secured his services in the summer of 1906.

The quick-raiding winger made his debut for the Robins in a 2-0 defeat at Everton in October 1906 before going on to provide a host of chances for the likes of Maxwell and Gilligan. That season, City finished runners-up in the First Division, three points behind champions Newcastle United.

The following season he helped the Ashton Gate club reach the FA Cup Final where they lost 1-0 to Manchester United. Staniforth was a first team regular for the Robins for five seasons, scoring 15 goals in 150 games before leaving the club to join Grimsby Town. After two seasons with the Mariners, Staniforth signed for Liverpool but managed only three league appearances with the Anfield club.

STEWART, BILLY

One of the main features of Billy Stewart's play was his exceptionally long throw-in, although his running and jumping technique was eventually outlawed. He first came to the fore when playing with the Black Watch team which won the Army Cup. Later while stationed with the Royal Scots Greys in Ireland, he was a member of the Belfast Distillery side which won the Irish Cup.

Preston North End bought him out of the army in 1890 and in three seasons with the Deepdale club, he made 70 league appearances. He joined Everton in the summer of 1893, forming part of the club's famous half-back line of Holt, Campbell and Stewart. He played in the 1897 FA Cup Final which the Blues lost 3-2 to Aston Villa. Midway through the following season, he left Goodison Park to become captain of Bristol City as they began to establish themselves as a professional club.

His first game for City came in a 1-1 draw at Millwall Athletic on the opening day of the 1898-99 Southern League season, a campaign in which the club finished runners-up. Injuries hampered his progress the following season, at the end of which he was forced to retire.

SUBSTITUTES

The first-ever Bristol City substitute was George Showell who came on for John Ateyo in a 2-2 draw at Manchester City on 28 August 1965. The club had to wait until 4 May 1968 for their first goalscoring substitute - Terry Bush scoring in the 4-2 win at Aston Villa. The greatest number of substitutes used in a single season by the Robins under the single substitute rule was 33 in season 1983-84. From 1986-87, two substitutes were allowed and in 1992-93 the club used 63. For the last few seasons, three substitutes have been allowed and in 1999-2000, 94 were used. Terry Cooper holds the club record for the most individual appearances as a substitute in one season with 20 in 1983-84. The greatest number of substitute appearances for Bristol City has been made by Wayne Allison who came on during 46 League games with eight more substitute appearances in cup-ties.

SUNDAY FOOTBALL

The first-ever Sunday matches in the Football League took place on 20 January 1974 during the three-day week imposed by the government during the trial of strength with the coalminers.

Bristol City travelled to Burnden Park to play Bolton Wanderers but lost 2-1 in front of a 23,315 crowd with Ernie Hunt scoring the Robins' goal.

SUSTAINED SCORING

In 1946-47, Don Clark set a new club record when he scored 36 goals in 37 League games for the Robins. He scored four goals in the wins over Aldershot (Home 9-0) and Torquay United (Home 5-0) as well as hat-tricks against Exeter City (Away 3-1) and Mansfield Town (Home 5-2). He also scored five goals in two FA Cup games including four in the 9-3 rout of non-League Hayes.

SWEENEY, GERRY

Glasgow-born full-back Gerry Sweeney began his career with Celtic but after being given a free transfer by the Parkhead club, he joined Morton. He spent five years at Cappielow Park, scoring 16 goals in 139 games and representing the Scottish League.

In August 1971, Bristol City manager Alan Dicks paid £22,000 to bring him to Ashton Gate where he scored on his debut in a 3-3 draw against Millwall on the opening day of the 1971-72 season.

He went on to be a regular member of the City side for the next ten seasons, being ever-present in four campaigns including 1975-76 when the club won promotion to the First Division. He also helped City win the Anglo-Scottish Cup in 1977-78 but in 1982 the 'Ashton Gate Eight' crisis forced his release. Sweeney, who had scored 27 goals in 456 League and Cup games for the club left to play for York City.

He then appeared for a number of non-League clubs before becoming player-manager of Clevedon Town. After a spell as Walsall's assistant-manager, he returned to Ashton Gate, first as a part-time coach and then as the club's assistant-manager to Joe Jordan.

T

TAINTON, TREVOR

A former England Schoolboy international, Trevor Tainton joined the club as an apprentice before turning professional in September 1965. Despite some impressive performances in the club's reserve side, he had to wait until September 1967 before making his league debut in a 1-0 home win over Carlisle United. It was 1969-70 before he established himself as a first team regular with the Ashton Gate club and the following season he was instrumental in the Robins reaching the League Cup semi-finals.

A skilful winger, he was ever-present when City won promotion to the First Division in 1975-76 and two seasons later he appeared in every game as the club won the Anglo-Scottish Cup. Unfortunately his career at Ashton Gate was eventually cut short by the financial crisis of 1982 when he became one of the 'Ashton Gate Eight'. Having scored 27 goals in 552 League and Cup games, he played out the rest of that 1981-82 season with Torquay United, making 19 league appearances for the Plainmoor club.

After playing for a number of non-League clubs, he now works as a security officer at Oldbury Power Station.

TAIT, ALEX

Alex Tait began his career as a part-time professional with Newcastle United, preferring to qualify as a schoolteacher rather than concentrate on a full-time career in the game. Tait spent eight years at St James' Park and though he only scored eight goals in 34 games in that time, they included a hat-trick in a 6-1 win over Sunderland when he deputised for Jackie Milburn.

Tait joined Bristol City in the summer of 1960 and played his first game for the club in a 4-0 home win over Barnsley. Forming a good striking partnership with John Ateyo, Tait reached double figures in each of his three full seasons with the club, netting a hat-trick in the 8-2 FA Cup win over Dartford in

November 1961. He went on to score 44 goals in 133 League and Cup games before being allowed to join Doncaster Rovers in the summer of 1964.

After just one season at Belle Vue he moved to non-League Burton Albion where he succeeded Peter Taylor as the club's player-manager.

TAYLOR, BOB

It was Dick Malone, a member of Sunderland's 1973 FA Cup winning side and manager of Northern League side Horden Colliery Welfare that recommended Bob Taylor to Leeds United where after netting a hat-trick in his first game for the juniors he was immediately offered terms. Unable to win a regular place in the Elland Road club's starting line-up, he left for Bristol City just before the transfer deadline in 1989 in an exchange deal involving Carl Shutt.

He was an instant success at Ashton Gate and in 1989-90, his first full season with the club, he was the Third Division's top scorer with 27 goals as the club won promotion. He continued to find the net on a regular basis the following season as the club sought to consolidate its position in Division Two. Taylor had scored 58 goals in 126 games for the Robins when in January 1992, West Bromwich Albion paid £300,000 for his services.

It was under new manager Ossie Ardilles that Taylor's Albion career really flourished, becoming the first Baggies' player to score as many as 37 goals (in all competitions) for over seventy years. Though lacking a certain amount of pace, Taylor makes up for it with great strength on the ball and a high workrate. He went on to score 113 goals in 281 games for Albion, playing his part in keeping the club in the First Division before joining Bolton Wanderers on a free transfer in July 1998.

He had spent two highly successful loan periods with the Trotters the previous season when his performances had already made him a great crowd favourite. The scorer of some vital goals for the Wanderers including two in the First Division play-off semi-final win over Ipswich Town, Bob Taylor left the Reebok Stadium in March 2000 to return to West Bromwich Albion.

TAYLOR, JOCK

Left-half Jock Taylor began his career with his home-town club Cowdenbeath before later playing for Raith Rovers. It was from the Stark's Park club that City manager Bob Hewison signed him in October 1927 but he had to wait six months before making his first team debut in a 1-0 defeat at Stoke. Following the arrival of Ernie Brinton from Avonmouth, Taylor switched to left-back and over the next six seasons, appeared in 157 games. Unfortunately most of this time was spent with the Robins struggling to avoid relegation to the Third Division (South) and in May 1934 he joined Halifax Town.

In his first season at the Shay, he almost helped the club to promotion but they had to settle for runners-up spot in the Third Division (North). Taylor later had a spell with Clapton Orient before returning to Ashton Gate. Unable to break into the first team, he went to coach Cork before holding a similar position with HBS in Holland.

THICKETT, HARRY

Harry Thickett began his playing career with Sheffield United in 1890 but two years later joined Rotherham Town before returning to the Blades in December 1893. He went on to play in 261 league games for United, appearing in three FA Cup Finals and winning full international honours for England. In May 1904 he moved to Bristol City, making his debut in a 3-0 win at Chesterfield early the following season. At the end of that campaign in which he played 14 games, he retired.

In March 1905 he had been appointed the club's manager and in 1905-06 his first season in charge, he led City to the Second Division title. Many club records were established that season - 30 League wins, 14 consecutive League wins, 24 League games without defeat and six consecutive away wins. In 1906-07, City finished runners-up in the First Division after blowing their chances of taking the title over Easter. In 1909, Thickett took Bristol City to the FA Cup Final where despite a spirited performance they lost 1-0 to Manchester United.

It came as a great surprise when in October 1910, Thickett was sacked. It is highly probable that he lost his job due to the internal strife at the club rather than the performance of his team. After leaving City, he moved to Trowbridge to run a pub.

THIRD DIVISION

Bristol City have had six spells in the Third Division. Their first in 1922-23 lasted just one season as the Robins won the Championship at the first attempt, finishing six points ahead of second placed Plymouth Argyle. However after just one season back in Division Two, City were relegated and in 1924-25 began their second spell in Division Three.

After finishing third that season and fourth in 1925-26, the Robins again won the Third Division (South) Championship, finishing two points ahead of runners-up Plymouth Argyle. In fact, that was the sixth successive season that the Pilgrims had finished runners-up in Division Three.

Five seasons of Second Division football followed before City were relegated, beginning their third spell in Division Three in 1932-33. This was the club's longest spell in the Third Division, 16 seasons either side of the Second World War before they won the Championship for a third time in 1954-55, finishing nine points clear of Leyton Orient.

Relegation in 1959-60 saw City embark on their fourth spell of Third Division football before they won promotion in 1964-65 as runners-up to Carlisle United. There followed 11 seasons of Second Division football before in 1975-76 the club won promotion to the First Division.

After four seasons in the top flight, City were relegated to the League's basement in three successive seasons, their fifth spell in the Third Division lasting just one season, 1981-82. Promotion followed in 1983-84 and the club began its last spell in Division Three the following season, eventually winning promotion in 1989-90.

THIRD DIVISION (SOUTH) CUP

The Third Division Cup competition began in season 1933-34, one for the North and one for the South. Bristol City's first match in the competition saw them soundly beaten 7-1 by Bournemouth whilst 1934-35 also saw them lose at the first hurdle as Watford beat them 4-1 at Vicarage Road. City won their first match in the competition the following season, beating rivals Bristol Rovers 4-2 before going out 1-0 at Bournemouth.

The Robins made another first round exit in 1936-37, losing 2-0 at home to Gillingham. In 1937-38, City went all the way to the final, beating Torquay United (Home 3-0) Cardiff City (Home 2-0) Walsall (Away 2-1) and Millwall (Home 2-0). In the two-legged final which was held over until the start of the following season, the Robins were beaten 6-1 at Reading but gained a little revenge with a 1-0 win in the second leg at Ashton Gate. In 1938-39 the last season of the competition, the Robins produced their biggest win with a 6-0 defeat of Cardiff City before losing 1-0 at home to Torquay United.

THRESHER, MIKE
One of six footballing brothers to play for Chard Town, his impressive performances led to Pat Beasley signing him for Bristol City in January 1954. When he arrived at Ashton Gate, Thresher was an inside-forward but Beasley saw his potential as a defender and he was converted to left-back. He made his league debut for the Robins in a 2-0 win at Reading the following December. After that, Thresher was a virtual ever-present for the next ten seasons, winning a Third Division (South) Championship medal in his first campaign with the club.

Thresher's only goal in 414 League and Cup appearances came in a 1-1 draw at Southend United in November 1963.

He had made seven appearances in the club's 1964-65 promotion-winning season after which he left to play non-League football for Bath City. He later rejoined Chard, finishing his career where he had started.

TINDILL, BERT
Yorkshireman Bert Tindill began his career with Doncaster Rovers, helping the Belle Vue club win the Third Division (North) title in season's 1946-47 and 1949-50. Tindill was the club's leading marksman in 1955-56 and scored 122 goals in 402 games before joining Bristol City for £8,000 in February 1958.

Tindill made his Bristol City debut in a 1-0 home defeat by Rotherham United and though it seemed that the club would be relegated, his ten goals in 14 games helped the Robins recover. His total included hat-tricks in the wins over Barnsley (Home 5-0) and Fulham (Away 4-3). Forming a prolific partnership with John Atyeo, Tindill, who was ever-present in 1958-59, had scored 31 goals in 59 games when he was allowed to return to Yorkshire and join Barnsley.

He helped the Oakwell club reach the fifth round of the 1960-61 FA Cup competition before leaving to play non-League football for Frickley Colliery.

TINNION, BRIAN
Versatile midfielder Brian Tinnion began his Football League career with Newcastle United and had made 37 first team appearances for the Magpies when Bradford City paid £150,000 for his services in March 1989. In four seasons at Valley Parade, Tinnion scored 27 goals, many of them spectacular, in 166 League and Cup appearances before leaving to join Bristol City for a fee of £180,000 in March 1993.

He made his debut for the Robins in a 2-1 defeat at Swindon Town but three games later scored his first goal for the club - the winner from the penalty-spot in the 2-1 defeat of Bristol Rovers. Since then Tinnion has showed his versatility down City's left side, playing at both full-back and in midfield and though injuries have restricted his appearances in recent seasons, he remains an important member of the Robins' first team, having scored 25 goals in 321 League and Cup games.

TOONE, GEORGE

Goalkeeper George Toone began his career with Notts County, appearing for the Meadow Lane club in their 1894 FA Cup Final success. He also helped County win the Second Division title in 1896-97 before leaving two seasons later to join Bedminster. Whilst with Notts County, Toone made two appearances for England against Scotland and Wales in 1892, being on the winning side on both occasions.

When Bedminster amalgamated with Bristol City in 1900, he became the club's first-choice 'keeper. In his only season with the club, he did not miss a single game, keeping 12 clean sheets as City finished runners-up in the Southern League. At the end of that campaign, Toone rejoined Notts County but two years later retired to become a publican in the town.

TORRANCE, SANDY

Glasgow-born left-half Sandy Torrance played his early football with Renfrew Juniors before Bristol City manager Joe Palmer signed him in the summer of 1921. He made his debut for the Robins in a 3-0 defeat at West Ham United in October 1921 and went on to play in most of that season's games. Though the club were relegated, Torrance helped them win promotion and the Third Division (South) Championship in 1922-23, scoring the final goal in the 3-1 win over Charlton Athletic that secured the title for the Ashton Gate club.

Torrance, who had been appointed the Robin's captain, was still with the club when they won the Third Division (South) Championship again in 1926-27 but after losing his first team place to Andy Smailes, he left to play non-League football for Bath City. Torrance, who had scored 10 goals in 176 games for the Robins died in tragic circumstances in an air raid on Bedminster in April 1941.

TOWNSEND, LEN

Len Townsend played his early football for Hayes before joining First Division

Brentford in the summer of 1937. During the Second World War, Townsend 'guested' for Belfast Celtic before returning to Griffin Park for the resumption of League football in 1946-47. He was the Bees' leading scorer that campaign but in the close season he followed Dai Hopkins to Ashton Gate.

He scored a hat-trick on his League debut for the Robins as Southend United were beaten 6-0 on the opening day of the 1947-48 season. Townsend, who formed a prolific goalscoring partnership with Don Clark, netted 31 goals in 39 games including four in a 6-0 home win over Norwich City. He continued to find the net on a regular basis in 1948-49, taking his tally of goals to 50 in 80 League and Cup games before joining Millwall.

He later played for Guildford City, helping the non-League club to reach two successive Southern League Cup Finals. After a spell back at Hayes as the club's player-coach, he played for Slough Town before ending his career with Maidenhead United.

TRANSFERS

The record transfer fee received by the club was the £1.75 million that Newcastle United paid for Andy Cole in March 1993.

The record transfer fee paid out by Bristol City was £1.2 million to Gillingham for Ade Akinbiyi in May 1998.

TUFT, BILLY

Strong-tackling full-back Billy Tuft began his career with Coseley United before joining Wolverhampton Wanderers in July 1896. He spent four seasons at Molineux, gaining top flight experience before joining neighbours Walsall in the summer of 1900. After just one season with the Saddlers, the reliable defender moved to Bristol City as the Ashton Gate club entered the Football League.

He made his debut in the club's first-ever game in the competition, a 2-0 win at Blackpool and over the next four seasons, was a virtual ever-present. When City won the Second Division Championship in 1905-06, Tuft played in the first five games of the season before losing his place to fast-emerging Joe Cottle.

Tuft who had appeared in 151 League and Cup games for the Robins was awarded a deserved benefit match against Southampton in February 1907.

U

UNDEFEATED
The club's best and longest undefeated sequence in the Football League is 24 matches between 9 September 1905 and 10 February 1906. This incorporated the club's best run of undefeated away matches, a total of 21 games between 16 September 1905 and 22 September 1906. City's best run of undefeated home matches is 25, between 24 October 1953 and 27 November 1954.

UNUSUAL GOALS
Bristol City 'keeper Ray Cashley was playing in a Second Division match against Hull City at Ashton Gate on 18 September 1973 when a clearance he made was assisted by a strong wind and went first bounce over the head of the visiting goalkeeper Jeff Wealands and into the Hull net. The Robins won 3-1.

UTILITY PLAYERS
A utility player is one of those particularly gifted footballers who can play in several different positions. Two of Bristol City's earliest utility players were Hugh Wilson and Alex Caie. Hugh Wilson appeared in every position except goalkeeper for City. A Scottish international and captain of Sunderland and Bedminster, he stayed when the latter club amalgamated with City. Caie too was a versatile player and like Wilson, was born north of the border. He was equally at home at full-back, half-back or inside-forward.

After the mid-1960s, players were encouraged to become more adaptable and to see their roles as less stereotyped. At the same time, much less attention was paid to the implication of wearing a certain numbered shirt. Some of the more versatile players came to wear all the different numbered shirts at some stage or another, although this did not necessarily indicate an enormous variety of positions. Gerry Harrison and Rob Edwards have worn a number of different outfield shirts, whilst Rob Newman appeared in all ten outfield shirts during his time at Ashton Gate.

V

VALLIS, FRANK
Goalkeeper Frank Vallis began his career playing for Horfield United in the Bristol Suburban League and after a number of impressive displays was asked to Ashton Gate for a trial. Turning out in a friendly against Bristol Rovers, he did enough to convince the City board that he was their man. He made his League debut in a 1-0 home win over Bury on the opening day of the 1919-20 season, the first season of League football after the First World War. Vallis was ever-present that campaign and again in 1920-21 when he kept a club record 24 clean sheets. Though the Robins were relegated the following season, Vallis was instrumental in the club winning the Third Division (South) Championship in 1922-23. Eventually displaced by Billy Coggins, Vallis, who had made 243 first team appearances, left Ashton Gate along with Charlie Sutherland to join Merthyr Town in June 1926. On leaving the Welsh side, he played non-League football for Yeovil and Petters.

VIALS, PERCY
Centre-forward Percy Vials began his career with his home-town club, Market Harborough before helping Kettering Town win the Southern League Championship in 1927-28. His performances attracted the attention of a number of clubs but while Leicester City were deliberating after Vials had a trial; with the Filbert Street club, Alex Raisbeck stepped in and paid £125 for his services in October 1928.

He scored twice on his City debut in a 6-0 home win over Oldham Athletic and ended the season as the club's joint-top scorer with Cecil Blakemore, both players netting 15 goals. Injuries and a loss of form restricted his appearances in 1929-30 but he returned to form the following season, scoring 12 goals in 18 games.

He had scored 37 goals in 78 League and Cup games when he joined First

Division Middlesbrough in May 1932. Unfortunately illness prevented him from winning a regular place at Ayresome Park and he left to play non-League football for Hinckley United and Atherstone Town.

VICTORIES IN A SEASON - HIGHEST

In 1905-06, Bristol City won 30 of their 38 league fixtures to win the Second Division Championship. They repeated the feat in 1954-55, this time from 46 matches as they lifted the Third Division (South) Championship.

VICTORIES IN A SEASON - LOWEST

The Robins' poorest performance came in 1931-32 when they won only six matches out of their 42 league games and finished bottom of the Second Division.

W

WADSWORTH, WALTER

Walter Wadsworth began his career with West Cheshire League club, Lingdale and then Ormskirk before joining Liverpool just before the First World War. Built more like a slim-line modern centre-half rather than the traditional hefty version, Wadsworth soon became a vital component in the Liverpool side that went on to win two League Championships during the early 1920s. Yet surprisingly he was never capped by his country. Always keen to sneak upfield, he scored eight goals in 240 games before following Alex Raisbeck to Bristol City in May 1926.

Appointed club captain, he made his City debut in a 1-1 draw at Gillingham on the opening day of the 1926-7 season. Missing just two games he helped the Robins to win the Third Division (South) Championship in his first season at Ashton Gate. His only goal for the club came the following season in a 3-0 home win over Fulham but at the end of that campaign after which he had played in 71 games, he returned to the north-west to join New Brighton.

WALSH, ALAN

After a series of impressive performances for Horden Colliery, Alan Walsh joined Middlesbrough but after just three substitute appearances for the Teeside club, he was allowed to join Darlington in October 1978.

In six seasons at the Feethams, Walsh scored 90 league goals, still the club record. In the summer of 1984, Walsh left the Quakers to join Bristol City for £18,000, a fee set by the Football League tribunal. The Hartlepool-born striker made his debut for the Robins in a 2-0 home win over Wigan Athletic on the opening day of the 1984-85 season, going on to top the club's goalscoring charts with 20 goals in 45 games. Forming a good understanding up front with Steve Neville, he helped the club reach two Wembley finals. In February 1987 he netted his only hat-trick for the club in a 5-0 home win over Doncaster Rovers.

He went on to score 88 goals in 257 League and Cup games before leaving to join Besiktas in July 1989.

After that he moved around, playing for Walsall, Glenavon, Huddersfield Town, Shrewsbury Town, Cardiff City and Hartlepool United. He is now Community Development Officer at Bristol Rovers.

WALSH, TOMMY

'Tot' Walsh began his Football League career with Bolton Wanderers, where he experienced top flight soccer with the Trotters. Unable to win a regular first team spot with the then Burnden Park club, he joined Bristol City for a fee of £1,500 in January 1924.

He made his debut in a 1-0 defeat at the hands of Bradford City and though he gave a number of impressive displays, he was unable to prevent the club being relegated to the Third Division (South). Walsh was the club's leading scorer for the next three seasons with a best of 32 in 39 games in 1926-27 when the Robins won the Third Division (South) Championship. His total included a club record six goals in the 9-4 win over Gillingham, four goals in the 5-0 defeat of Watford and a hat-trick in a 7-3 win at Aberdare Athletic.

He had scored 91 goals in 150 League and Cup games when he was allowed to leave Ashton Gate and join Crystal Palace in May 1928.

He almost helped the Selhurst Park club win promotion in his first season but Charlton Athletic pipped them to the Third Division (South) title on goal average. On leaving the league scene, he returned to his native Lancashire to see out his career with Hurst.

WAR

Bristol City lost a number of players fighting for their country. During the First World War, goalkeeper Tommy Ware died on the Western Front in 1915 and Edwin Burton, who scored four goals in 13 games towards the end of the 1914-15 season, was also killed in action.

WARD, JOHN

John Ward was a regular goalscorer with Lincoln City, netting 91 in 240 League games for the Sincil Bank club and helping them win the Fourth Division Championship in 1975-75. In the summer of 1979 he followed former Imps boss Graham Taylor to Watford. Unable to establish himself in the first team at

Vicarage Road, his career seemed to go into decline afterwards. He was Taylor's assistant-manager at Aston Villa before leaving to take charge at York City.

His first season in charge at Bootham Crescent was unspectacular but the Minstermen got off to a great start in 1992-93. Unable to maintain this form, the club faded and early the following season, Ward was offered the manager's post at Bristol Rovers. He spent three seasons at Twerton Park with a best finish of fourth in Division Two in 1995-96.

In March 1997, he was appointed manager of Bristol City, the club finishing the campaign in fifth place in Division Two. Ward's first full season in charge, 1997-98, saw the Robins win promotion to the First Division as runners-up to his old club, Watford.

However, in October 1998 after City had won just three of its first 16 league games, Ward ended 18 months in charge by walking out on the club.

WARE, TOMMY

Goalkeeper Tommy Ware was home on leave from the army at Christmas 1911 when he was called up to replace the injured Harry Clay in the match at Hull City, which the Robins lost 3-0. He played in another four games that season before leaving the forces and playing on a more regular basis for the next two seasons. His spell of 26 games in 1912-13 was also as a result of an injury to Clay who damaged a leg in a goalless draw at home to Blackpool. His performances towards the end of that season resulted in City managing to avoid the Second Division re-election zone. In 1913-14 he was the club's 'keeper for the second half of the season, replacing Howling. Ware, who had made 57 appearances for City was one of the first to be called up when war was declared because of his previous military experience but sadly he was killed in action in June 1915.

WARTIME FOOTBALL

In spite of the outbreak of war in 1914, the major football leagues embarked upon their planned programme of matches for the ensuing season and these were completed on schedule at the end of April the following year. City finished 13th in Division Two and went out of the FA Cup in the second round to Everton. The following season the club participated in the South West Combination but following the decision of Portsmouth and Southampton to join the London Combination, the League folded. The Robins then played friendly matches until midway through the 1917-18 season when the Bristol County Combination was formed. City emerged as champions in the first year of the competition, winning one of their matches 14-2 against RAF (Filton). However, perhaps the most significant development during the years of the First World War occurred in March 1917 when the club purchased Ashton Gate following the expiry of the lease.

In contrast to the events of 1914, once war was declared on 3 September 1939, the Football League programme of 1939-40 was immediately suspended and the government forbade any major sporting events, so that for a while there was no football of any description. City had opened the season with a 1-0 win at Aldershot before losing 2-1 at home to Norwich City and drawing 3-3 with Brighton and Hove Albion. Various League and Cup competitions were eventually organised, though City struggled to put out a side. They did however reach the third round of the War League Cup in 1942-43 but lost 2-1 on aggregate to Aston Villa. During the hostilities, the Number One Stand at Ashton Gate was badly damaged, being hit twice by enemy bombers.

WATKINS, JOHNNY

An England Youth international, Johnny Watkins began his League career with Bristol City, making his first team debut in a 3-1 win over Norwich City in September 1953. Despite playing well and holding his place for the next game, a 5-0 defeat at Swindon, it was another three seasons before he returned to first team action. After that Watkins was a regular in the City side. His powerful shooting brought him a number of important goals with a best return of 10 in 43 games during the 1957-58 season. The flying winger went on to score 21 goals in 105 games before surprisingly being allowed to join Cardiff City for £2,500 in the summer of 1959.

He scored on his debut for the Bluebirds in a 3-2 home win over Liverpool and went on to be the Welsh club's only ever-present as they won promotion to the First Division as runners-up to Aston Villa, scoring 15 goals in his 42 appearances. Midway through the following season, he left Ninian Park to join Bristol Rovers in a deal which saw Dai Ward sign for the Bluebirds. He seemed to lose his form at Eastville and after making just 23 league appearances, drifted into non-League football first with Chippenham Town and then Welton Rovers.

WATNEY CUP
This was Britain's first commercially sponsored tournament and was a pre-season competition for the top two highest scoring teams in each division of the Football League, the previous season. But clubs could only compete if they had no other European involvement.

After two Bobby Gould goals helped the Robins beat Peterborough United 2-1, City lost 4-1 at Stoke in the semi-final, the Potters going on to beat Hull City in the final.

WAUGH, KEITH
Goalkeeper Keith Waugh joined his home-town club Sunderland as an apprentice before turning professional in the summer of 1974. Unable to break into the Wearsiders' first team, he moved to Peterborough United on a free transfer and in five seasons at London Road, made 195 league appearances for 'The Posh'. His performances led to Sheffield United paying £80,000 for his services in August 1981. Waugh helped the Blades' rise from the Fourth to the Second Division before injuries and a loss of form cost him his place. There followed loan spells with Cambridge United and Bristol City before Robins' manager Terry Cooper signed him on a permanent basis in July 1985.

Waugh had made his City debut in a 4-3 win over Plymouth Argyle on Boxing Day 1984 but following his transfer, was virtually an ever-present. He helped the club to two successive Freight Rover Trophy Finals at Wembley, winning the first against Bolton Wanderers in 1986 and losing to Mansfield Town on a penalty shoot-out in 1987. In 1987-88 he helped City reach the play-offs but in August 1989 after appearing in 201 League and Cup games, he joined Coventry City for £40,000.

He later played for Watford before ending his involvement with the game and joining the police force.

WEATHER CONDITIONS
On Saturday 1 September 1906, Bristol City entertained Manchester United on what is thought to be the hottest day a League programme has ever been completed - the temperature was over 90F(32C). Walter Bennett gave the Robins a 1-0 lead after five minutes when he scored from the penalty spot. However, United hit back to win 2-1 with goals from Picken and Roberts.

WEDLOCK, BILLY

The club's most capped international, Billy Wedlock played his early football for local club Melrose before helping Arlington Rovers win the Bristol and District League title in 1898-99.

He joined Bristol City in 1900 and played his first game for them in a 2-0 win at Queen's Park Rangers in the Western League. However, in those days his chances were restricted and after just one more first team appearance, he left to play for Aberdare Athletic. He stayed for four seasons, helping his new club win the South Wales Cup and reach the Welsh Cup Final.

In 1905, Bristol City manager Harry Thickett persuaded Wedlock to return to Ashton Gate and in his first full season back with the club, helped them win the Second Division Championship.

Wedlock was the club's first-choice centre-half for the next 11 seasons, helping them to runners-up in the First Division in 1906-07 and to the FA Cup Final against Manchester United in 1909. Wedlock who represented the Football League, the Professionals and Gloucestershire, won the first of his 26 full caps for England on 16 February 1907 in a 1-0 win against Ireland at Goodison Park.

Standing only 5ft 5ins but weighing 10st 7lbs, he was known as 'Fatty' Wedlock but his other nickname of the 'India-Rubber Man' was more apt, for Wedlock was most likely to 'bounce up' in attack and defence!

Though he played his last international match against Wales at Ninian Park in March 1914 when he scored in a 2-0 win, he was still in the City line-up when league football resumed in 1919. Playing the last of his 393 League and Cup games against Hull City on 11 September 1920, Wedlock then retired to become licensee of the Star Inn opposite the main entrance to Ashton Gate.

WELCH, KEITH

Finding it difficult to break into the league side of his home-town team, Bolton Wanderers, goalkeeper Keith Welch joined Rochdale in March 1987. He was ever-present in three consecutive seasons for the Spotland club including 1989-90 when he helped 'Dale reach the fifth round of the FA Cup for the first time in their history. He had played in 239 games for Rochdale when Bristol City paid a record £200,000 for his services in the summer of 1991.

After making his Robins' debut in a 1-1 draw at Southend United on the opening day of the 1991-92 season, Welch held off the challenge from Sieb Dykstra,

Phil Kite, Andy Leening and Steuart Naylor to be the club's first-choice 'keeper for the next six seasons. Welch was between the posts when City beat Liverpool in the 1993-94 FA Cup third round replay at Anfield and was instrumental in the club reaching the Second Division promotion play-offs in 1996-97.

One of the best goalkeepers in the Football League with the ball at his feet, Welch appeared in 318 first team games for the Ashton Gate club before being out of contract in the summer of 1999, and joining Northampton Town where he won the club's 'Player of the Year' award.

WELSH CUP

Bristol City won the Welsh Cup for the only time in their history in 1933-34, beating Tranmere Rovers 3-0 in a replay at Sealand Road after the first match at Wrexham's Racecourse Ground had been drawn 1-1. In 1961-62, the Robins lost 2-0 at home to Cardiff City in the sixth round, it was the only time since the war that Bristol City had taken part in the Welsh Cup.

WHITE, JACK

A former miner, centre-half Jack White played his early football for Frickley Colliery before being given the chance at league level by Aldershot in 1944. During his first few seasons at the Recreation Ground, White made the majority of his appearances at centre-forward and by the time he moved to Bristol City for a fee of £5,300 in October 1952 he had scored 24 goals in 209 games for the Shots.

After making his City debut in a 4-0 home win over Gillingham, his performances at the heart of the defence meant there was no way back for Dennis Roberts who was forced into retirement. White was appointed club captain and in 1954-55, his third season at Ashton Gate, he led the Robins to the Third Division (South) Championship.

White went on to score 11 goals in 227 League and Cup games before joining non-League Cambridge City as player-manager. He later took charge of Wellington Town before ending his involvement with the game.

WHITEHEAD, CLIVE

A former England Youth international, Clive Whitehead joined the Robins from West Midlands club, Northfield after impressing for them against City in an FA Youth Cup tie. After working his way up through the ranks, he made his league debut at Millwall in October 1973, scoring in a 2-0 win. After scoring the goal that defeated Portsmouth to ensure the club's promotion to the First Division in 1975-76, Whitehead missed just one game the following season as City finished 18th in the top flight.

A regular member of the City side for seven seasons, he was successfully converted into a left full-back and went on to score 14 goals in 256 League and Cup games before the club's worsening financial position forced them to sell him to West Bromwich Albion for £100,000.

After overcoming some difficult times, Whitehead was appointed the Baggies' captain but after they had failed to win immediate promotion to the First Division following their relegation the previous season, he was given a free transfer and joined Portsmouth.

He made 73 appearances for the Fratton Park club but after a loan spell with Wolves he moved to Exeter City, helping the Grecians win the Fourth Division title in 1989-90.

He later held the position of player-manager at Yeovil Town before returning to Ashton Gate as coach.

WILLIAMS, ALAN

One of the club's most outstanding post-war discoveries, centre-half Alan Williams made his debut for the Robins in a 3-1 defeat at Blackburn Rovers in February 1957. His early performances for City almost led to him winning Under-23 recognition for England but he just missed out when the game against Scotland was cancelled because of bad weather ! Throughout all the seasons of the club's struggle to avoid relegation from the Second Division, Williams was outstanding at the heart of the City defence. Sadly, the inevitable happened and after the Robins were relegated to the Third Division in 1959-60, Williams, who had scored two goals in 149 games, joined Oldham Athletic for £1,000.

He captained the Latics to promotion from the Fourth Division in 1962-63 when he was ever-present. After four years at Boundary Park, he signed for Watford but couldn't settle at Vicarage Road and after a spell with Newport County, moved to Swansea in October 1968 for £1,500.

He starred in the Swans' Fourth Division promotion-winning season of 1969-70, but in June 1972 after scoring seven goals in 145 league games, he left the Vetch Field to play non-League football for Gloucester City. Williams later managed Keynsham Town and Almondsbury Greenway.

WILLIAMS, BERTIE

Welsh international inside-forward Bertie Williams joined City from Merthyr Tydfil in the summer of 1926 but had to wait until Christmas Eve 1927 before making his first team debut in a 3-1 win at South Shields. He struggled to win a regular place in the City side during his first two seasons at Ashton Gate but in 1929-30 he missed very few games and ended the campaign as the club's top scorer with 17 League and Cup goals including a hat-trick in a 4-1 home win over Nottingham Forest.

His form that season led to him winning full international honours for Wales when he played against Northern Ireland in Belfast in February 1930. Williams had scored 30 goals in 114 games for City when he left to join Sheffield United in January 1932.

He spent five seasons at Bramall Lane, appearing for the Blades in the 1936 FA Cup Final but left the club in the summer of 1937 following a dispute over terms.

WILLIAMS, BOBBY

Nicknamed 'the Shadow' because of his ability to get through the opposition defence, inside-forward Bobby Williams joined the Ashton Gate club as a junior. He made his debut for the Robins in April 1959 in a 1-0 defeat at the hands of Leyton Orient. However, over the next couple of seasons, Williams only made 11 league appearances though he did score five goals.

It was 1960-61 before he established himself as a first team regular, forming a prolific striking partnership with John Ateyo. His best season in terms of goals scored was 1961-62 when he netted 21 in 45 League games. The following season he scored four goals in the 5-2 win at Halifax Town and a hat-trick in the 6-3 defeat of Southend United.

Williams, who scored four goals in the first eight games of the club's promotion-winning season of 1964-65, had netted 81 times in 212 League and Cup games when in February 1965 he moved to Rotherham United.

After two seasons with the Millmoor club he returned to Bristol to play for Rovers but left after just 27 appearances and joined Reading. On leaving the league scene, he signed for Southern League Weymouth Town but sadly a car accident forced him to retire. He later rejoined Reading as youth team manager.

WILLIAMS, CYRIL

Local-born inside-forward Cyril Williams joined the Ashton Gate club in May 1939 but because of the Second World War had to wait over seven years before making his league debut for the Robins. During the hostilities, he 'guested' for Reading and Spurs, eventually making his League debut in the 4-3 defeat at Aldershot on the opening day of the 1946-47 season. His impressive displays in the City side, which included a hat-trick in a 3-1 win at Mansfield Town, brought the scouts to Ashton Gate and in the summer of 1948, he joined West Bromwich Albion.

He helped the Baggies win promotion to the top flight in his first season at the Hawthorns but after three seasons with the club, Williams, who had scored 19 goals in 71 games, rejoined Bristol City.

He netted his second hat-trick for the Robins in a 5-0 home win over Crystal Palace in September 1952, later helping the club win the Third Division (South) Championship in 1954-55. He went on to score 78 goals in 318 League and Cup games before joining non-League Chippenham Town as player-manager in 1958. Williams, who later took charge at Gloucester City, was tragically killed in a car crash in January 1980.

WILSON, HUGH

Hugh Wilson was born at Mauchline, Ayrshire in 1869 and began his career with the Newmilns club. He joined Sunderland in 1890 and made his debut in the club's first-ever game in the Football League when they lost 3-2 at home to Burnley. Wilson stayed with the Wearsiders for nine years, playing mainly as a half-back before later moving to play in the forward line. Wilson scored some important goals and netted a hat-trick in a 3-0 home win over Bury in October 1898. A versatile player, Wilson also appeared at full-back and on one occasion kept goal ! He captained Sunderland in most of his 258 appearances before leaving to play for Bedminster in May 1899.

Appointed captain, he made his debut for Bedminster at Sheppey United on the opening day of the 1899-1900 season, scoring one of the goals in a 2-0 win. A Scottish international, he stayed with the club when they amalgamated with Bristol City and in 1900-01 appeared in all ten outfield positions, scoring 13 goals in 45 games. Included in that total were hat-tricks against Gravesend United (Home 6-0) and Tottenham Hotspur (Home 4-1). Wilson, whose long throw-ins were a feature of his game, later returned to Scotland to play for Third Lanark.

WIMSHURST, KEN
Half-back Ken Wimshurst began his career with Newcastle United before moving to Gateshead where he made his league debut. Wolverhampton Wanderers signed him but he failed to make the first team at Molineux and in the summer of 1961 he joined Southampton for a fee of £1,500.

Wimshurst had been recommended by scout Bill Rochford and the Saints had cause to thank him, for the South Shields-born wing-half went on to give Southampton six seasons good service. His best spell came in the club's FA Cup run of 1962-63 when he played in all seven games and scored in the victories over York City and Nottingham Forest. A clever passer of the ball, he left The Dell after making 171 League and Cup appearances to join Bristol City for £12,000.

He made his debut for the Robins in a 1-0 defeat at Rotherham United in November 1967, holding his place for the remainder of the season. A virtual ever-present in the City side, he was an influential member as the Robins reached the League Cup semi-finals of 1970-71. Wimshurst went on to score 10 goals in 165 League and Cup games before becoming the Ashton Gate club's assistant-coach in July 1972. Two years later he succeeded John Sillett as City's chief coach before following a stint coaching in Egypt he briefly assisted Don Mackay at Dundee. Wimshurst now runs Southampton's School of Excellence in Bath.

WORST START
The club's worst-ever start to a Football League season was in 1933-34. It took 14 league games to record the first victory of the season, drawing five and losing eight of the opening fixtures. The dismal run ended with a 5-1 success against Cardiff City at Ninian Park on 11 November 1933 with Gordon Reed scoring two of the goals.

WRIGHT, BOB
Glasgow-born defender Bob Wright's career was wrecked by the war. After impressing for Horden Colliery Welfare, he joined Charlton Athletic and after making his debut at Portsmouth in October 1938, he made 28 appearances before the outbreak of the Second World War. He made 47 wartime appearances for Charlton and 19 for Middlesbrough but retired in 1947.

On hanging up his boots, he became assistant-manager to Jimmy Seed at The

Valley but in April 1949 he left to take over as manager of Bristol City. Though he signed a number of new players including Alec Eisentrager and Arnold Rodgers, City had a mediocre season, finishing 15th in the Third Division (South). Wright complained that he was not given a free hand and in June 1950, he resigned because of this.

He later had a spell as assistant-manager to Bert Tann at Bristol Rovers.

WYLIE, TOM

Outside-right Tom Wylie began his career with his home-town club, Maybole in Ayrshire before being signed by Rangers. He spent three seasons with them during which time he won Scottish international honours when he played against Ireland. Wylie also played for a Glasgow select team against the likes of Edinburgh, London and Sheffield. On leaving Ibrox, he came south of the border and after spells with Everton and Liverpool, he joined Bury.

He helped the Shakers win the Second Division title in 1894-95 and then promotion to the top flight after they had beaten his former club Liverpool 1-0 in the Test Matches. After a couple of seasons playing in the First Division, Bristol City manager Sam Hollis signed him as the club turned professional in 1897.

He made his City debut in the club's first game in the Southern League, a 7-4 home win over Wolverton. Though this was his only season with the club, he scored 19 goals in 31 games including four in the 9-1 FA Cup first qualifying round win over Clifton. At the end of the campaign he hung up his boots and became a Football League referee.

X

'X'

In football 'x' traditionally stands for a draw. The club record for the number of draws in a season occurred in 1919-20, 1965-66 and 1982-83 when the Robins drew 17 of their matches.

XMAS DAY

On Christmas Day morning 1941, Bristol City set off to play at Southampton in a wartime regional match. They were dispersed in three cars. The last to leave contained two players and the team's kit. This arrived first but although the referee delayed the kick-off, there was no sign of the missing vehicles. Southampton offered five reserves plus their trainer who had not played for years and a side was assembled with the aid of a soldier, a schoolmaster and another spectator.

The match started an hour late and 20 minutes after the missing nine had arrived. One car had a puncture, the other came to its aid and they all lost their way afterwards!

At half-time the Bristol City team tried to sneak Ernie Brinton into the game as he was not unlike one of the deputies playing. They rubbed mud over him but he was quickly spotted by an alert linesman and sent back to the dressing room. Southampton won 5-2 although their trainer scored against his own club!

Two Bristol City players have scored hat-tricks on Christmas Day. They are Bert Neesam in a 3-2 win over Grimsby Town in 1914 and Tot Walsh in 1926 when City beat Aberdare 7-3 on their way to winning the Third Division (South) Championship. The club played their last league game on Christmas Day in 1957 when two goals from John Ateyo helped City beat Derby County 2-1.

Y

YOUNG, BOB
A former Scottish junior international, right-back Bob Young played his early football with Vale of Eden and Dundee Violet before City manager Harry Thickett persuaded him to join the Ashton Gate club. Replacing Archie Annan he made his debut for the Robins in a 1-1 home draw against Newcastle United in September 1907.

Forming an effective full-back partnership with England international Joe Cottle, he helped City reach the FA Cup Final in 1909 where they lost 1-0 to Manchester United. Following the arrival of John Kearns from Aston Villa, Young switched to right-half but still couldn't get on the scoresheet! He was still a member of the City side when league football resumed in 1919-20. At the end of that season, Young, who had appeared in 172 League and Cup games, retired and took up refereeing in the Bristol Suburban League.

YOUNGEST PLAYER
The youngest player to appear in a first-class fixture for Bristol City is Nyrere Kelly who played in the Fourth Division match against Hartlepool United (Away 1-3) on 16 October 1982 when he was 16 years 244 days old.

YOUTH CUP
Bristol City have reached the FA Youth Cup Final on just one occasion and that was in 1972-73. Their opponents in the two-legged final were Ipswich Town who beat the Robins 3-0 at Portman Road and drew 1-1 at Ashton Gate to take the trophy 4-1 on aggregate.

Z

ZENITH

Though the club have won the Third Division (South) Championship on three occasions, reached an FA Cup Final and won the Sherpa Van Trophy and Anglo-Scottish Cup, few fans will argue over which moment has been the finest in the club's history.

In 1905-06, the Robins won the Second Division Championship in what was only their fifth season in the Football League. That season, the club suffered only two defeats in 38 matches. They won 30 and drew six of their games. Thirty-one of their 66 points came from away fixtures which produced 13 wins and five draws. They also won 14 consecutive league matches.

ZENITH DATA SYSTEMS CUP

The Zenith Data Systems Cup replaced the Simod Cup for the 1989-90 season. Bristol City first participated in the competition in 1990-91 but after drawing 1-1 at Oxford United after extra-time, lost 3-2 in the resultant penalty shoot-out. In 1991-92, the Robins fared no better, losing 2-1 at home to Southampton, so failing to win a match in their two years in the competition.

BIBLIOGRAPHY

Let's Talk About Bristol FC - Tom Morgan
Sentinel Publications, 1946

Bristol City: The Complete History of the Club - Peter Godsiff
Wensum, 1979

Bristol City: A Complete Record 1894-1987 - David M.Woods and
Breedon Books, 1987 - Andrew Crabtree

Bristol City FC The First 100 Years - Leigh Edwards and David M.Woods
Sansom and Co., 1997

ACKNOWLEDGEMENTS

I should like to express my thanks to the following organisations for their help: Bristol City Football Club, the Association of Football Statisticians; the Football League; the British Newspaper Library; Bristol Central Reference Library; and the Harris Library;
Thanks also to the following individuals: Ben Hayes; Iain Price; Frank Atkins and George Hadfield.

PHOTOGRAPHS

The photographs in this book have been supplied by the Lancashire Evening Post and from the author's personal collection.